THE WAR IN SOUTHERN AFRICA

An Analysis of South Africa's Total National Strategy (1948–1994)

MIGUEL JÚNIOR

authorHOUSE

AuthorHouse™ UK
1663 Liberty Drive
Bloomington, IN 47403 USA
www.authorhouse.co.uk
Phone: 0800.197.4150

© 2018 Miguel Júnior. All rights reserved.

No part of this book may be reproduced, stored in a retrieval system, or transmitted by any means without the written permission of the author.

Published by AuthorHouse 07/09/2018

ISBN: 978-1-5462-9497-9 (sc)
ISBN: 978-1-5462-9495-5 (hc)
ISBN: 978-1-5462-9496-2 (e)

Print information available on the last page.

Any people depicted in stock imagery provided by Getty Images are models, and such images are being used for illustrative purposes only.
Certain stock imagery © Getty Images.

This book is printed on acid-free paper.

Because of the dynamic nature of the Internet, any web addresses or links contained in this book may have changed since publication and may no longer be valid. The views expressed in this work are solely those of the author and do not necessarily reflect the views of the publisher, and the publisher hereby disclaims any responsibility for them.

Contents

Acronyms and Initialisms ix
Acknowledgments xi
Abstract xiii
Introduction xv
Methodology xvii
Preface xix

PART I

Chapter 1

The Total National Strategy of South Africa 1
The Strategic Atmosphere in Southern Africa 1
The Political Grounds of Strategy 4
The Guiding Lines of the Total National Strategy 24
The National Security Situation 24
Factors Which Influence the Total National Strategy 26

PART II

Chapter 2

The Two Fundamental Strategies 31
The External Political Strategy 31
The Political Strategy of Defence 44
The Strategic Doctrines 54

PART III

Chapter 3

The Evolution of War and the Changes..63
The Modality of Strategic Action 63
The Strategic Change and the End of Apartheid 66

Conclusions...69
Bibliography...71
About the Author 79

In loving memory of Filomena Centeno.

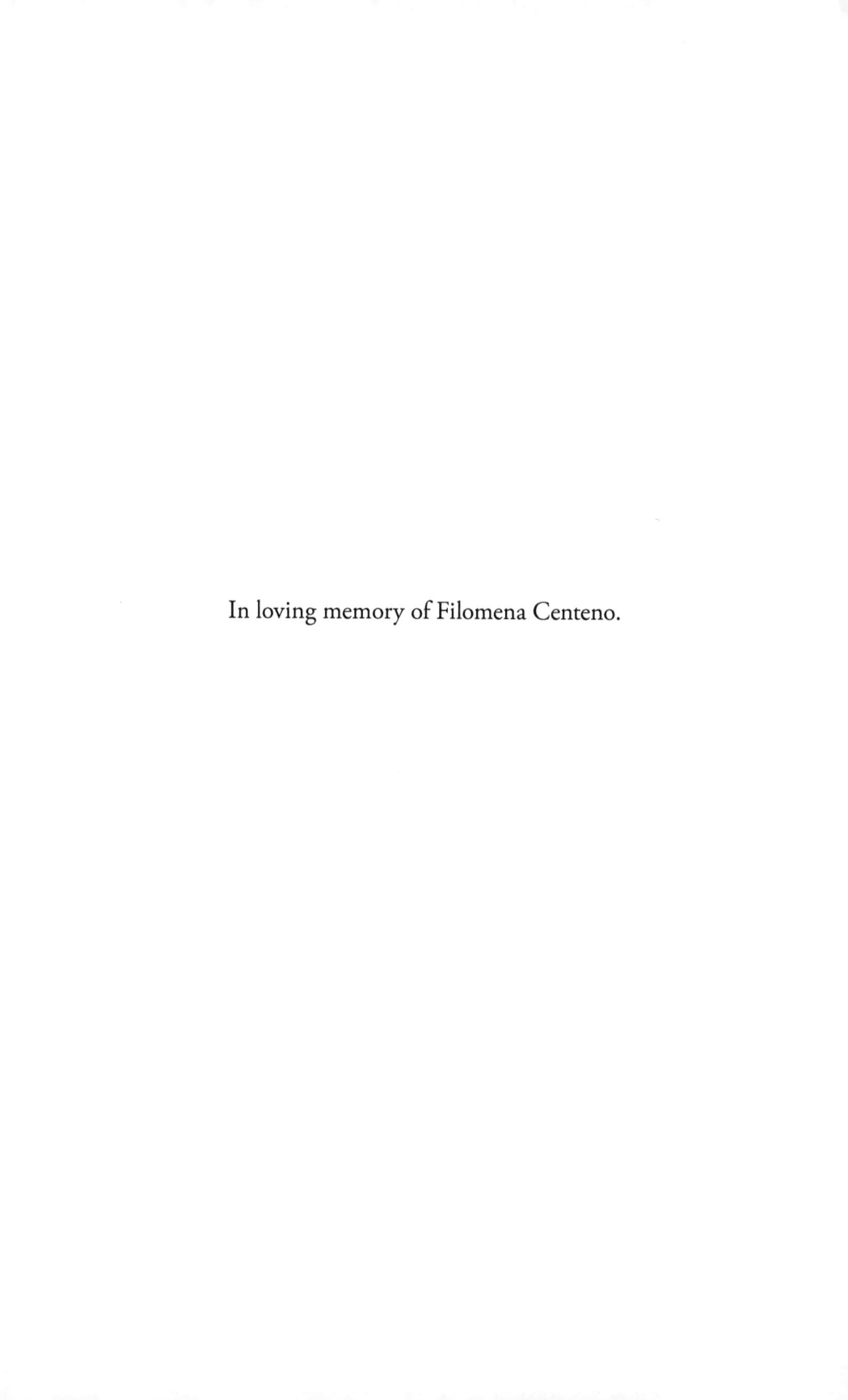

Acronyms and Initialisms

ADD	—	Archives of the Defence Department
ANC	—	African National Congress
FNLA	—	National Front for the Liberation of Angola
FRELIMO	—	Front for the Liberation of Mozambique
MPLA	—	People's Movement for the Liberation of Angola
NATO	—	North Atlantic Treaty Organisation
OAU	—	Organisation of African Unity
PAC	—	Pan Africanist Congress
PLAN	—	People's Liberation Army of Namibia
SADCC	—	Southern African Development Coordination Conference
SADF	—	South Africa Defence Forces
SANDC	—	South Africa National Documentation Centre
SANDC	—	South Africa National Defence College
SACP	—	South African Communist Party
SWAPO	—	South West African People's Organisation
UN	—	United Nations
UNITA	—	National Union for the Total Independence of Angola
ZANU	—	Zimbabwe African National Union
ZAPU	—	Zimbabwe African People's Union

Acknowledgments

I want to thank the people who helped me achieve my goal. Works of this scope have peculiarities that include traveling abroad, hours of research, and analysis of data. It is a stringent type of research, but at the same time it is rich because the researcher faces important multidisciplinary data that is helpful in widening the knowledge of readers. Such research also places useful information of great historical relevance in the hands of readers.

I thank engineer José Eduardo dos Santos, former president of the Republic, as well as the general Hélder Vieira Dias, for support they gave in launching the project. I also acknowledge to Dr Aldemiro Vaz da Conceição and lieutenant-general António Santana Lungo for their attention and for the way they streamlined the process.

Throughout the time that it took to complete this project, I counted on the help of other people. Hence I thank the staff of the South Africa National Documentation Centre (SADC), Defence Department Archives (ADD), the library of the South African National Defence College (SANDC), the political science department of the University of Pretoria, and the military chancellery of Angola in South Africa. Finally, I thank my family and friends for their understanding and the support.

Miguel Júnior

Abstract

In Southern Africa, there was a war between the Republic of South Africa and other states of the region (Mozambique, Lesotho, Zimbabwe, Botswana, Zambia, Tanzania, and Angola). It fell within the scope of the more general confrontation of the Cold War, but it has its own traits and differs greatly from other wars that occurred on the African continent in the second half of the twentieth century.

The nature of this war can be understood only from an examination of the historical background and from an analysis of the national strategies of each belligerent state. Examination of the national strategies of the belligerent states makes it possible to identify in concrete terms how each state organised itself for war and how it used force. National strategies imply the use of force in the context of relations between states, especially when opposing interests are at stake.

That is why, in this strategic study, we have analysed the strategic thinking of South Africa's overall national strategy and its general guidelines, as well as its doctrines. In the end, we examined the outcome of the battle. Therefore, this research study looks exclusively at South Africa's overall national strategy.

Keywords: war, Southern Africa, Angola, South Africa, Cold War, strategies, apartheid, politics, diplomacy, defence, security, doctrines, nuclear deterrent, limited war.

Introduction

The present is the past transmuted. It is indispensable to dive deeply into the past to unearth many facts that deserve to be known in detail. Southern Africa experienced one of the most significant armed conflicts during the second half of the twentieth century. It affected the whole region. This is the truth. And now is the time to deepen studies concerning it.

Studies about an armed conflict may be carried out from several perspectives. But the idea herein is to study the armed conflict of Southern Africa from the perspective of studies on war. Hence, and given that a war may be studied in three dimensions, this analysis fits into the strategic dimension. What is at stake is the study of a national strategy of a concrete state. This work studies the strategic thought of South Africa and its total national strategy (1948–94).

The year 1948 is the initial milestone of that strategic thought because it was the year when the National Party, based on Afrikaner nationalism, took political power and established the apartheid system. As such, this analysis has to do with the total national strategy of the South African state monopolised by the Afrikaner minority.

This study about the total national strategy of South Africa is structured practically because historical, political, economic, diplomatic, international, defence, and security issues are involved. It is conceived in conformity with strategic culture and theories based on universal strategic thought. But it is based mainly on the strategic thought and culture of South African political power that was in force from 1948 to 1994. In this line of reasoning, the data that supports this study is mostly from South African sources and, essentially, official and state documents. This documentary support grants coherence and credibility to the work.

This analysis of the total national strategy of South Africa is divided into three parts and has three chapters. In the end there are conclusions and a list of documentary sources. Finally, we believe that we have contributed to better knowledge of the strategic thought of South Africa in 1948–94.

Miguel Júnior

Methodology

The focus of our research is analysis of the total national strategy of the Republic of South Africa in 1942–94. We have analysed fundamental aspects of the political, diplomatic, and military activities of the Republic of South Africa. Under the rules of studies on war, we have also studied moral, economic, social, cultural, and technical scientific issues. From a military point of view, we parsed the data on military budgets, troops, national military efforts, and the use of military strength relative to other states of Southern Africa, especially the People's Republic of Angola. But we also considered the military alliances forged by this belligerent state to make war.

Hence, this study about the total national strategy of South Africa fits into the strategic dimension of analysis, as this is the first step towards interpreting a war. But we have examined the total national strategy of this state on the basis of its official documents and in conformity with its national policies and its conception of national security. The total national strategy of South Africa is described on the basis of assumptions inherent to strategic processes.

Beforehand, we had to consider that the accumulated experience of modern states shows that the national strategy of a state is associated with its need to prepare national power, regardless of its capacities, and to try to apply it to conquer and ensure maintenance of national aims, whether remote or immediate, in conformity with the grounds expressed in their constitutions. The formulation of a national strategy has implications that require a state to make choices in accordance with challenges of the present context, to determine whether it needs more security or more development, or to combine both options. Regardless of the choices made, a national strategy, meaning that national strategies are always at the service of the same purpose, represents a target to be reached by a state.

National strategies are conceived to attend to situations that arise from interactions that states establish, varying from peace to war. On this basis, and given that our study topic is about armed conflict (war), we incorporated in the body of the text other considerations that prove indispensable. Still, the formulation of a national strategy has implications linked to its preparation, its materialisation, and the use of its results. Formulation of a national strategy requires collecting data. We assumed that South Africa acted accordingly in preparing its total national strategy.

In order to improve its understanding of strategic matters and to formulate its vision of national security, South Africa held a symposium on national security in Pretoria on 31 March and 1 April 1977, by initiative of the University of Pretoria.[1] We therefore excluded studies, assessments, and strategic surveys about this state and others in the period under analysis. We took into consideration only historical, political, economic, military, and national security factors.

This study also entailed understanding the impact of war from a political, economic, social, and cultural point of view within South African society because comprehension of a war requires going beyond the battlefields. Hence we included a discussion of changes in South Africa and Southwest Africa.

These methodological considerations guided this work.

---

[1] "The purpose of this symposium is to try to determine and describe the broad problem area ('operational universe') of modern policymakers and decision-makers in government on the subject of national security and then to examine what the broad policies, action guidelines and appropriate strategies in each of the conventional areas of action, and their effective co-ordination towards a relevant national security policy are and should be. These role players are individuals and institutions on all levels of government, which, of course, include both the political and administrative dimensions of intelligent action." *National security: A modern approach*, ISSSP, 1978.

Preface

The southern part of the African continent is a vast zone of undefined contours that, starting at the Cape, extends to the Congo and Rovuma Basin, covering the whole of Angola. It has been a strategic area for many centuries. The greatest African powers formed in that area, such as Congo kingdoms, Monomotapa, and, more recently, the Zulu Empire. There some of the most violent rivalries that marked the continent were born. Multiple reasons exist to explain this.

The first is linked to geostrategic maritime communications. Southern Africa controlled the only maritime route between Europe and Asia until the opening of the Suez Canal in the late nineteenth century. That is why the European powers created their main points of support on the continent there. The process began with the Portuguese, who established a special relationship with Congo, the origin of modern Angola, when they built their main base on the island of Mozambique in the sixteenth century and advanced on Zambezi.

Shortly afterward, the Dutch had a more strategic vision and occupied the Cape, which became the focus of the European presence due to its climate and its strategic location at the junction of two oceans.

In the nineteenth century, the British, aware of the importance of the Cape to global navigation, took the Dutch's place, causing the Boer to advance to the interior of the continent. Germany, too, when it became interested in the creation of a colonial empire in the nineteenth century, settled on the Atlantic coast (southwest South Africa) in the Indian Ocean (German East Africa), for a connecting point for its colonies in Asia and the Pacific. France, finding the main positions already occupied, settled in Madagascar. In short, all powers with global ambitions except the US sought support points in Southern Africa.

The second reason, equally geographic, is linked to special climatic conditions of Southern Africa. With a large area of temperate climates, including the presence of great plateaus, rivers that are navigable almost all year round, irrigated and broad valleys, and favoured communications, Southern Africa is an area particularly favourable for human habitation.

The third reason is subsoil riches. In the nineteenth century, the African continent had weight in terms of subsoil products on the world market in only three products: diamonds, gold, and ores from Katanga. All were in Southern Africa, and gold production was the most important worldwide. In the twentieth century, when multiple strategic rare minerals emerged, especially uranium, most of that was found in Southern Africa, too, and nowhere else on the continent.

The fourth reason is historical and cultural. Southern Africa had long been a meeting point between African powers, India, and the Islamic world, with slave trading and trading networks dating back to the first millennium or even earlier. The formation of the great African powers also led to large-scale migrations of African populations, which peaked at the time of the expansion of the Zulu Empire in the nineteenth century. The arrival of the Europeans—first the Portuguese, then many more—turned the situation even more complex because, adding to the existing clashes and rivalries, now there were clashes between European powers. For centuries, Southern Africa has been a meeting point for cultures, religions, and powers of three continents, facilitated by its complex and overlapping maritime, fluvial, and terrestrial communication networks.

The fifth reason is historical and is linked to the race to Africa in the late nineteenth century. The race to Africa began in Southern Africa, when the scheme prepared by Great Britain to control Congo's trade failed, which gave rise to the Berlin Conference. It was mainly about confrontations and clashes in Southern Africa, which is not surprising, because great mineral riches and many diverse communities were there. Among them was the largest focus of European presence on the continent. Angola and Mozambique were at the forefront of this race to Africa. Their centres controlled the inland passageways: the Congo and the Benguela corridor on the side of Angola, and the corridors of Lourenço Marques (Maputo) and Beira from the Mozambique side. These were the contradictory solutions that led to the creation of modern Angola and Mozambique, which set the boundaries still in place today.

The sixth reason is linked to characteristics of colonization and decolonization in this part of the continent. On the one hand, no other region of the continent has created a racist regime like that of South Africa following the Anglo-Boer War—the largest war in sub-Saharan Africa to this day. Although South Africa had a broad autonomy that would lead to one of the first formally independent states on the African continent, its racist regime meant that colonialism continued to exist. This regime was one of the hardest forms of colonialism, particularly being exercised by a minority of the population against the vast majority rather than by a power from another continent.

However, with this book, Lieutenant General Miguel Júnior presents another step in its maturation process. He leaves the ground that unfolded in the recent history of Angola to launch a theoretical flight in the field of great foreign strategy, based on South Africa's *total strategy*, the most powerful international agent in Southern Africa.

It was a careful and pertinent choice. South Africa, during the first nine decades of the twentieth century, is a fascinating case study. First of all, it is one of the few states that officially declared that it had a *total strategy*, that is, a coordinated and interconnected approach at all levels of action (internal and external) to achieve priority objectives, to which everything else was subordinated. What makes it particularly interesting is that these ends were essentially of an internal order. What South Africa saw as the main purpose was the international legitimation of the apartheid regime as an essential step towards its internal consolidation. The fact itself was not then new, for to a certain extent all external strategies have implications in the internal order and aim at consolidating the power that promotes them. What was new was for this to be stated clearly as the central goal of a total strategy. This is more remarkable in that it was a march against the current, a coordinated effort to preserve a type of society that received almost universal condemnation, as votes in the United Nations proved.

In this march against the current, South Africa had several advantages that allowed it to go beyond what was expected. The first was its economy—the strongest and most developed on the African continent—as well as access to a range of strategic products in the international system, from uranium to rare metals. The second advantage was the existence of two other regimes in Southern Africa that, while not racist, also intended to counter dominant tendencies in the international system and to maintain their status despite the international condemnation expressed by the United Nations. Those regimes were the Portuguese colonies and Rhodesia (Zimbabwe). The third advantage was that everything happened in the context of the Cold War, where the great powers knew that it was a zero-sum game, which strongly conditioned their action. This was particularly true as the USSR increased its importance in Southern Africa, forcing the United States to subordinate its strategy for the region to the logic of the global confrontation of the Cold War's final phase.

General Miguel Júnior draws attention to an original aspect of South Africa's total strategy: the creation of a limited nuclear arsenal. At the time it was a secret, detected early by the USSR, USA, and other powers. The South African strategy in this field was directly inspired by France's theory regarding the use of nuclear deterrent. The French doctrine was this: In the event of a serious threat to the state and to society involving the possibility of its destruction or occupation, an international warning would be made about the preventive use of nuclear weapons as a deterrent. If this warning was not enough to deter the aggressor, the threat would escalate, and a tactical nuclear warhead would be used against a carefully chosen military target, one away from urbanized areas, in order to convince the aggressor of France's determination and to deter the continuation of its advance, paving the way for a negotiated solution. A third step would be a larger tactical nuclear attack, reaching goals at the aggressor's centre. If this failed, the option of using the strategic nuclear arsenal remained, the last resort, and would necessarily have extensive consequences.

With this doctrine, France became the first *autonomous* nuclear power, that is, with a distinct logic of the two great nuclear powers, which implied a different technology of its own. Its position inspired Israel to create a limited nuclear arsenal. Even today, Israel's official position is based on not denying nor confirming the existence of nuclear weapons, but it is generally accepted that it has an arsenal of a few dozen warheads and appropriate vectors for their use, including missiles, airplanes, and submarines with cruise missiles. The Israeli doctrine is equally original, although it is not public, which is understandable given that the official existence of the nuclear weapon is not recognized.

The South African nuclear program was a sign of weakness. The total strategy adopted contradicted trends in the evolution of the international system, which would be increasingly difficult to apply over time and could create a situation in which South Africa, understood as the apartheid regime, was threatened by its continuation. In other words, one could create a situation where the conventional pressure on borders, coupled with internal opposition, was too strong to be contained by conventional means. This idea was linked to another, which was the need to maintain the external threat far from the borders through active intervention against its bases and support points in Southern Africa, particularly in Angola.

The South African nuclear program began in the energy field in 1948, with the goal of building nuclear power plants that would be an alternative to oil since its import could be banned. At the time, South Africa was not yet thinking of a more directly military dimension.

As General Júnior points out, South Africa's President de Klerk officially stated that the nuclear military program started on 25 April 1974, following Portugal. Other sources note that the decision was taken earlier, possibly in 1973. The USSR followed the project and even proposed a pre-emptive strike at the US's uranium enrichment plant (known as the Y plant), which they rejected. The first test of a South African A-bomb took place in September 1979, in the ocean far south of the Cape.

South Africa in the 1980s was able to obtain six nuclear warheads. Their main problem was weakness in the vectors for their eventual use.

South Africa did not have usable ground-to-ground missiles, and the only device able to launch a tactical nuclear device was the Buccaneer, of British origin. South Africa received sixteen Buccaneer S50s from 1965, but the arms sale embargo, which was imposed shortly thereafter, entailed a rapid depletion of the force, with growing problems obtaining spare parts. The device was used in raids in Angola starting in 1975, being the only one capable of reaching targets far from the border and carrying a significant amount of weaponry. It became normal for some of the best Buccaneers to be reserved for the nuclear program—possibly since 1982, when South Africa got A-bombs that could be launched by Buccaneers.

The author points out that during negotiations in the late 1980s, South Africa suggested that if they come to an agreement, it would use a nuclear weapon against Luanda. It was not a vain threat. The South African regime had this capacity, with six nuclear warheads ready to be used. The threat itself, veiled and indirect, never publicly and officially made, is equally understandable within South Africa's doctrine. According to this, in case of a serious threat and in the impossibility of resisting pressure with conventional means, the threat of using the nuclear arsenal was the first step of the escalation. Its purpose was to make the other side yield and agree on acceptable terms. If this did not happen, there was still an intermediate step, which was the use of a warhead against a limited target. It would be normal for a military target far from the urban zone to be chosen in order to lessen expected international condemnation. The fact that South Africa decided that the target could be Luanda (Angola's largest city and its political centre, where more than 10 per cent of the population lives) shows the anxiety behind the final negotiations. In verbal terms, South Africa decided to jump a step and threaten Luanda directly for maximum effect.

The South African regime was fully aware that the resolution of the "Angola problem" was an essential step towards finding a way out into the alley where the total strategy had cornered it. It knew it was playing its last rounds, and it was a race against time, so it did not hesitate to move to the maximum threat level, always in a veiled and unofficial manner, of course. Interestingly, also on the Angolans' side, it was understood that this was a race against time, particularly because the USSR had already hinted that it was not willing to continue the level of recent support indefinitely. Angola negotiated from a position of strength, after the final phase of the Cuito Canavale campaign, but with serious limitations that made it equally desirable for an effective solution in the short term, even as a way to allow the internal evolution of South Africa, in order to end apartheid.

In this context, what is the real impact and effect of the South African's nuclear threat? It is too early to say, not only in terms of sources but also of testimonies. We do not know, for example, what the real South African military plans were if negotiations had failed. It is one of the many question marks in the recent history of Southern Africa.

In any case, the implications of these developments upon international relations are immense. They illustrate one of the most complete cases of building a total strategy over many decades, where everything plays together from social, economic, cultural, diplomatic, and military policies, among others. It was an effort to prolong for an extended period an abnormal situation, one condemned by the international community, through a military strategy of open intervention abroad. It also illustrates how a nuclear doctrine can be inserted in this thinking, with the concern of creating a *last ratio*, a destabilizing factor that could change the rules of the game, an asset that was kept for an emergency remedy or for final negotiations.

With this work, General Júnior takes an essential step in his personal evolution and in modern Angolan historiography. Having deepened Angola's situation through a series of important writings, the author understands that he needs a more comprehensive view of Southern Africa and that this will be accomplished through the study of the South African strategy as one of the most significant long-term agents in this process. By means of this study, the author innovates in theoretical terms, particularly in strategic theory and international relations. Its most significant advances relate to understanding the South African total strategy theory as it integrates a doctrine regarding the use of nuclear weapons for essentially political and military purposes.

One observation relates to the whole work of General Júnior, but is explicit in this work. Just as we speak of a South African total strategy, we can also speak of a total strategy of Angola, or to be more exact, of the government of Luanda, as other agents of Angola are involved. The subject, which deserves further reflection, was a long-term strategy—pragmatic, flexible, always imaginative, and even surprising and innovative. It always involved a difficult balance on a tightrope, involving great powers with much greater capacities than Luanda. That government can brag about being the only one to successfully manage a decades-long process with many twists and turns and low punches, a difficult articulation between internal and external levels, and between social, economic, diplomatic, and military levels, among others. General Júnior's vision of the process eventually imposed itself. Extraordinarily, it happened during an intense civil war, leading to a new basis of national unity. These long decades of war, terrible and devastating to Angola, were the end of the birth in the midst of fire and fury of an African nation. Apartheid South Africa claimed to have a total strategy. It did, but it failed. On the other hand, the government of Luanda succeeded in its own total strategy, even without officially naming it. It is difficult to find in Africa another example of such a lasting, firm, flexible, pragmatic, and *victorious* leadership, something that—although in Europe it is often not understood as such—is essential.

General Júnior must be congratulated, not only because he was an agent in this process, as one of the many millions of Angolans who committed themselves passionately and completely, but also because, with his post-peace work, he helps us better understand what happened and to have a more detached view, far from ideology and, above all, far from prejudice—a vision of history.

António José Telo
Professor of the Military Academy of Portugal
Lisbon, August 2017

CHAPTER 1

The Total National Strategy of South Africa

This chapter is about the strategic atmosphere and political influences that provided the political grounds for the strategy designed by South Africa during the era of its apartheid regime. It also covers lines of support for that total national strategy.

The Strategic Atmosphere in Southern Africa

To understand influences upon the strategy of Southern Africa, one must dive into the international strategic atmosphere of the region. In the second half of the twentieth century, this resulted from World War II, which configured a bipolar world where the United States of America and the Soviet Union led incontestably. On this basis, the military blocs NATO and the Warsaw Pact were formed to defend their interests. Furthermore, the conflicting ideologies of capitalism and socialism were the main ingredients for the positioning of political forces in different geographic areas.

The capitalist-oriented bloc tried to uphold values that arose from capital and its liberal, democratic political model. Those with the opposite view aimed to preserve socialism and its identifying traits, intending to expand the socialist camp and bring to its causes the subjugated, oppressed, and colonised peoples. On this basis, the socialist camp and the left-wing forces helped national liberation movements, the communist parties, the worker and union movements, and forces associated with these in several parts of the world. The bipolarisation of the world was a real and undeniable fact. It dictated alignments and was the main point of reference.

At the same time, another perspective arose in the context of international relations due to disputes between the two dominant blocs. This led to the foundation of the Non-Aligned Movement by a group of countries, which aimed to congregate forces outside NATO and the Warsaw Pact. Due to its nature, the Non-Aligned Movement included countries of socialist orientation and others of different views. As such, the Non-Aligned Movement emerged as another force in favour of the more general causes of oppressed peoples, peace, progress, and world stability.

Given the worldwide confrontation arising from the Cold War and its ideological struggle, regional configurations were established with their own political, economic, diplomatic, and military challenges. On this basis, states have devised bilateral and multilateral relations between them, privileging the ideological orientation and common political and economic interests. At the margin of the global confrontation arising from the Cold War were matters concerning international relations that affected all states under the United Nations charter.

One topic of conflict was the overthrow of colonial systems in Africa and Asia. It was said that colonial empires should be overthrown. This matter gained traction in the 1950s and 1960s as the world saw, slowly but steadily, the overthrow of some colonial empires. This was evidently due to efforts by the United Nations and some colonial powers that wished to move on to another stage of development and grant autonomy to native peoples. Hence, independent states were born in Africa and Asia from 1950 onward. States emerged, some from political struggle and others by armed struggle, as was the case of Algeria. But one colonial power—Portugal—was reluctant to decolonise its territories. It sought devices and was scarcely interested in heeding the claims of the elites and cultural and political movements of the territories under its jurisdiction, as was also the case with Angola.[2]

---

[2] Douglas Wheeler and René Pélissier, 2009, 193–230.

While the United Nations fought to put an end to colonial systems, in Africa a problem emerged that jeopardised the human condition, namely the emergence of the apartheid system in South Africa, which was established by the National Party in 1948 (David Welsh, 2009).[3] This system of racial segregation gained form and force due to the stands of the National Party and its followers. In parallel, South Africa opposed the United Nations resolutions that encouraged granting independence to the peoples of southwest Africa whose territory had been under its jurisdiction since the end of the First World War. Due to its stance, South Africa became isolated and was the object of international sanctions.

By the mid-1960s, many African states were already independent and became members of the United Nations and the Organisation of African Unity. Very little remained to be decolonised; the Portuguese colonies formed most of what remained. Moreover, Angola, Mozambique, and Guinea-Bissau chose armed struggle since the early 1960s as Portuguese colonialists maintained control of their overseas territories. Another critical situation concerned Rhodesia. This country had been at war since 1965 due to the strong positions of the regime of Ian Smith and its alliance with the racist regime of South Africa.[4]

In the situation that prevailed in the African continent in the last colonialist pockets, the Organisation of African Unity, through its National Liberation Committee, established as priorities the overthrow of the last colonial pockets, the struggle against apartheid, and the granting of independence to the peoples of southwest Africa.[5]

These facts and the interests of the liberation movements—ANC, FNLA, FRELIMO, MPLA, UNITA, SWAPO, ZANU, and ZAPU on one side and South Africa, Portugal, and Rhodesia on the other side—were the elements that influenced the strategic atmosphere in Southern Africa. But when the bases were established for the decolonisation of Angola and Mozambique between 1974 and 1975, South Africa forged

---

[3] David Welsh, 53–109. Rodney Davenport and Christopher Saunders, 377–396.
[4] Brian Raftopoulos and Alois Mlambo, 141–66.
[5] Manuel Martins Lopes, 1991, 57.

its plans and altered its strategic conduct.[6] Moreover, the collapse of the Portuguese colonies in Southern Africa and their independence in 1975 altered the balance of power in Southern Africa (Hermann Giliomee, 2012).[7]

The Political Grounds of Strategy

South Africa is a country in Southern Africa. It lies in the southernmost part on the Atlantic and Indian Ocean coasts and occupies an important geostrategic position. But to understand the total national strategy of South Africa, it is essential to dive into its political history.

The historic roots of South Africa are linked to the local communities of Khoisan peoples who lived in the region long ago and African peoples who settled in that space later, due to the waves of Bantu migrations from Central Africa (Rodney Davenport and Christopher Saunders, 2000, pp. 3–20). A core of Dutch explorers associated with the Eastern India Company of the Netherlands settled in the Atlantic coastal region in 1652, where they established a supply outpost, creating conditions that allowed that core to evolve until the emergence of the colony of the Cape. Interactions between the Dutch and local communities continued well into the seventeenth century. But Europe faced political and economic transformations in the last quarter of the eighteenth century that forced the British, who had the greatest naval power at the time, to take Cape Town (Leonard Thompson, 2014, p. 33). They took control of that strategic point due to their interests in the east and to prevent the French presence in the region.

Once installed in the colony of the Cape, and despite clashes with the Dutch and African communities, the British tried to develop the

---

[6] Luís Barroso, 2012, 35.
[7] Hermann Giliomee, 2012, 571. This author also stresses, on page 54, that the "Angolan adventure was a great humiliation and terminated the effort to win African friends through military intervention." From his point of view, that meant "that the balance of power had been disturbed since Angola, and that South Africa was no longer strongest power [in Southern Africa]."

region considering their interests. Besides, in the early eighteenth century, British colonial expansion took its first steps, and Afrikaners pursued their territorial conquest efforts.[8] But relations between the African communities and the British colonisers deteriorated in the second quarter of the eighteenth century. That led to military action. Nevertheless, the British, with their military action, conquered more lands and expanded their dominion.[9] Meanwhile, the progress of British colonialists and the occupation of lands altered the way of life of African societies, which caused wars and favoured the emergence of other kingdoms. In the wars, and due to other factors, the Zulu Kingdom stood because it held a well-orchestrated military strength and huge lethal force. This condition led that kingdom to invade, dominate, and dissolve other African kingdoms in different geographic areas of the territory in question.[10]

But the wars between African communities caused damages, dissolved those societies, and forced the dislocation of populations to geographic locations removed from their origins. Those wars provided white men with an "unprecedented opportunity" and allowed them to progress towards the eastern part of the territory.[11] Moreover, Afrikaners had been unhappy with British authorities since the 1830s because they lost part of their properties in the border wars against African communities. Given the generalised dissatisfaction felt among Afrikaners and their wish to own their businesses in spaces far from the "limits of the British colony", they left Cape Town in 1840 and went to fertile and sparsely populated lands. That displacement was known as the Great Trek.[12]

The Great Trek of Afrikaners to other places implied clashes and confrontation with the Zulus. The most significant clash between the

---

[8] The word *afrikaner* has to do with the people who, during the nineteenth century and earlier, were referred to as Dutch or Boer. According to David Welsh (2011, vii), that gentile adjective was first used in current language in the twentieth century.
[9] Leonard Thompson, 2014, 75.
[10] Idem, 84–86.
[11] Idem, 87.
[12] Idem, 88.

parties was the Battle of Ngome (Blood River) (Ian Knight, 1988, pp. 35–50).[13] In this battle, the Zulus suffered defeat because of the firearms of the enemy.[14] But as Afrikaners settled in new regions, they immediately created bodies to manage their political, military, and economic interests. Later, those bodies evolved and gave rise to the independent Afrikaner republics.[15] Meanwhile, Afrikaners from the Great Trek immediately established a dividing line from the African, Asian, and coloured population segments because they believed that this separation attitude was an "order from God".[16]

Due to the "territorial expansion" of Afrikaner emigrants in the nineteenth century, British authorities took measures to contain their impulses. But British demands faced the impositions of the counterparty, which culminated in an understanding between British and Afrikaners. The latter thus became "free and independent". Due to that understanding and to other dynamics, British settlers created another colony, the colony of Natal, with characteristic features.[17] In the late nineteenth century, the territory was formed by African independent regions, British colonies, and Afrikaner states. Nevertheless, those states were "inexorably part of the informal British Empire".[18]

Leonard Thompson explains that South Africa in 1870 "was an imbroglio of peoples with a disparity of origins and cultures: African, Asian and European. Irresolvable conflicts about lands and work were heightened by different ideological assumptions and contradictory perceptions that generated tensions in each community."[19] In such conditions, a British military force succumbed before the Zulus in the Battle of Isandlwana in 1879, which was a hard blow against British

---

[13] See *Great Zulu Battles 1838–1906*.
[14] Leonard Thompson, 2014, 91.
[15] Rodney Davenport and Christopher Saunders, 2000, 77–95.
[16] Leonard Thompson, op. cit., 92.
[17] This colony's traits came from having three communities within its territorial space in the 1870s: Africans, whites, and Indians. Meanwhile, Indians began arriving in the region in the nineteenth century due to decisions of the British Empire.
[18] Idem, 109.
[19] Idem, 109.

prestige.[20] Despite the defeat, the British pursued their struggle against the Zulus until the Zulu Kingdom disintegrated and stayed under British law.

With the discovery of diamonds and gold, Southern Africa became another engine of world economy. Exploitation of those resources accelerated economic life and became the root of new internal dynamics. British settlers obtained dividends from existing resources, while Afrikaners maintained their states and profited from an African workforce in favour of their economic interests. Economic progress was notorious, but that progress also increased the racial divide and opposition between parties. Then came the First War between British and Afrikaners in the late nineteenth century (1880–81).[21] The Afrikaners of the region of Transvaal won this war because they rebelled against the British.[22]

But because disagreements between parties did not cease with that war, Afrikaners again joined efforts, enlisted troops, acquired weapons abroad, and attacked the British. The British saw the attitude of Afrikaners as a "Second War for the Freedom of Afrikaners" (1900–02) (Thomas Pakenham, 1988).[23] This war, limited to the early twentieth century, was an authentic failure for the Afrikaners. Still, the Afrikaners' defeat had significant impact and created a number of problems that shook the whole community. Victory enshrined British supremacy and led to the Peace of Vereening agreement.[24] In these circumstances, all suggested absence of pressure from the Afrikaners, as they were the object of "incorporation in the force of the British Empire".

---

[20] See *Great Zulu Battles 1838-1906*, Ian Knight, 1998, 98–125.

[21] In this period, and more concretely from 1880 to 1881, the First Anglo-Boer War was fought. Arthur Conan Doyle, in his work *The Great Boer War*, explains these wars in detail. His work is the result of all that he witnessed during that period.

[22] The reason for the war has to do with the fact that the British, since the 1870s, were interested in annexing the region of Transvaal with the aim of establishing a "federated Stade within the British Empire". That British stance collided with the Afrikaner interests. British defeat in that clash became a symbol for Afrikaners.

[23] Thomas Pakenham explains in his work *The Boer War* the set of military events until peace was achieved.

[24] Leonard Thompson, 2014, 141–43.

In 1907, meanwhile, the situation changed greatly because Afrikaner communities pursued their struggle for a more comfortable position on the terrain. The colony of Transvaal, already part of the British Empire, again went under Afrikaner control. This allowed installing a system of self-government. The same happened with the colonies of River Orange and Cape, as Afrikaners were a majority in those places and had many adepts to their cause. But the colony of Natal stayed out, as this colony identified much more with the imperial ideals of Great Britain. Due to those gains, the territorial spaces free from British management joined efforts to deter British "imperial interference". In 1907, the British in turn made concessions based on an agreement signed with the Afrikaners. In these conditions, the parties conceived a draft constitution for the Union of South Africa, that is, United South Africa.[25] They sketched their draft in 1908, in a convention in Durban. But they took steps that led to the formation of the Union of South Africa without the presence of Africans. The latter were simply excluded from the concertation orchestrated between British and Afrikaners.

Once the constitution of the Union of South Africa was approved by the British Parliament, without major amendments, it came into force.[26] But in that constitution, they enshrined "four principles" that, according to Leonard Thompson, determined "the course of history of South Africa".[27] The first principle, which was inscribed in the constitution, established that the Union of South Africa should follow the "British model, creating a unitary State with a sovereign parliament.... [T]he four colonies became provinces of the Union of South Africa, but the Government legally prevailed over all local institutions. However, the [local] powers were not divided with the centre."[28] That is the point at which local governments, mainly those that were Afrikaner-based, took advantage of that constitutional standard to revert the situation

---

[25] This project would congregate the territories of the colonies of Cape, Natal, Transvaal, and the Free State of Orange.
[26] The British Parliament approved the constitution, with no significant amendments, in 1909.
[27] Leonard Thompson, 2014, 180.
[28] Idem, 150.

in their favour, as happened after one year. Hence, in the first semester of 1910, Louis Botha, ex-leader "of the military forces of the Afrikaner Republics", became the prime minister of the Union of South Africa, as a British dominion.[29] Although they depended on Great Britain, that Afrikaner feat left the South African British astonished because they saw the Afrikaner project within the framework of internal struggles between parties.

With the emergence of the Union of South Africa, we shall now examine the most significant military and economic developments to ease understanding of subsequent evolution. From a military point of view, the parties that formed the government of the Union of South Africa committed to create the Union Defence Force. They designed the present military force based on former troops of the parties and the implied interest of establishing a military organisation based on the Western models of the time. Although they established the Union Defence Force, the British maintained their military forces on the ground. There was a permanent force of the Royal Navy of Great Britain. But British military presence was understood in different Afrikaner circles as "military and constitutional dependency" of the Union of South Africa on the British Empire (van der Waag, 2015, 78).

Due to that tense relation, the parties' representatives were involved in clashes on several occasions. The differences persisted, and the anti-British attitude of Afrikaners continued until the First World War broke out in 1914 and beyond. The Union of South Africa took part in that war due to its condition of British dominion, as did the other countries that were members of the British Commonwealth. Therefore

---

[29] Under the pressure exerted on Britain in the nineteenth century for the country to grant autonomy to the territories that it held, Britain established the status of dominion for certain territorial spaces that it held. A British dominion, as was the case of the Union of South Africa since 1910, had self-government in its territory and extensive independence in matters of foreign affairs in the relation established with the imperial power. A British dominion was therefore also an autonomous community with strong bonds to the British Empire. British dominions, as was the Union of South Africa, were represented, that is, they had seats, in the League of Nations.

the military forces of the Union of South Africa were employed in the theatres of operations of France, Egypt, and Palestine.

In 1918, when the First World War ended, the defence force of the Union of South Africa took control of the defence of the country because the British military forces withdrew from the South African territory.[30] Meanwhile, missions assigned to the military forces of the Union of South Africa gave the green light for their intervention in Southern Africa, where there was a possession of the German colonial empire. Due to this situation, and given the direction of the struggle and the alliances that had formed and included the results thereof, the German possession—Southwest Africa—came under the direct control of the British. Hence the Union of South Africa was tasked with expelling the German forces that were in Southwest Africa to exert control of this territory. The defence force of the Union of South Africa executed that task.

Given the consolidation of white power, meanwhile, Africans founded the African National Congress (ANC) in 1912 with the aim of defending their interests. But two years after that achievement by the Africans, in 1914, the Afrikaners created the National Party (Christi van der Westhuizen, 2007).[31] The foundation of this party was meant to "protect the economic and cultural interests of Afrikaners and dissociate the Union of South Africa from the [British] Empire".[32] Given the political and economic internal dynamics, in 1924 the National Party and the Labour Party formed an electoral pact and won the elections against the South African Party. Nevertheless, the British Parliament decided to acknowledge all its dominions as independent territories in 1931, as was the case of the Union of South Africa.

---

[30] Ian van der Waag, 2015, 93.

[31] The National Party emerged by initiative of general JBM (Barry) Hertoz. Christi van der Westhuizen explains that "Hertzog had advocated for segregation as a 'permanent solution' before 1910. See *White Power & the Rise and Fall of the National Party*" (2007, 11). Proceeding, he highlights that the "foundation of the National Party represented the onset of political organization of Afrikaner nationalism." (Idem, 12.)

[32] Leonard Thompson, 2014, 158.

Since that political coalition took power, and until 1933, however, it did everything to safeguard the interests of Afrikaners and provide favourable conditions for them, to the detriment of Africans.[33] However, the political dynamic and the clash of interests created other facts that gave rise to the emergence of a governmental coalition called the United Party, formed by the National Party and the South African Party. In parallel, the political setting saw the arrival of another party, namely the Purified National Party, formed by Afrikaner militants and the pro-British Dominion Party (Ivor Wilkins & Hans Strydom, 2012).[34]

Five years later, in 1938, the United Party again won elections by a landslide, beating the Purified National Party and the Dominion Party. Despite that victory, the political conflict worsened in the United Party due to the war in Europe and the fact that Britain declared war on Germany in 1939. Despite differences within the party and society, the Union of South Africa was involved in the Second World War as an ally of Britain (Christopher Somerville, 1988).[35] Between 1940 and 1945, the military forces of the Union of South Africa were employed in theatres of operations in Africa and Europe. Besides, the involvement of the Union of South Africa in the Second World War represented a gain for the alliance and significant "strategic and economic input to the allied cause" since South African products were channelled to war.[36]

In 1921, a group of intellectuals founded the South African Communist Party (SACP) in the territory of the Union of South Africa. The African National Congress (ANC), which had emerged in the political arena in 1912, ultimately lost strength and weakened around 1930. Still it was the object of deep restructuring throughout the 1930s. Nevertheless, in mid-1940, with the creation of the party's

---

[33] Idem, 161.
[34] The Purified National Party was dominated by a "secret society of Afrikaner elite—farmers, businesspeople, clergy, teachers and academicians". This secret society was called *Broederbond*. Its history is described in the work *The Super–Afrikaners Inside the Afrikaner Broederbond* (Ivor Wilkins & Hans Strydom, 2012).
[35] Christopher Somerville (1988) describes South African participation in his work *Our War: How the British Commonwealth Fought the Second World War*.
[36] Leonard Thompson, 2014, 177.

Youth League, ANC radicalised due to stances taken by members Nelson Mandela, Oliver Tambo, and Walter Sisulu. In time, and due to the conditions of the struggle, the Communist Party of South Africa and the African National Congress established an alliance to better lead the fight against apartheid because the political system in force in the Union of South Africa represented "a special type of colonialism" (Alan Wieder, 2013).

Besides, racial segregation and discrimination were evident facts in society. Those practices much favoured whites to the detriment of Africans. On the other hand, urban and industrial growth were other realities, and there was progress in the mining and agricultural sectors. But these economic and industrial gains much heightened discrimination against Africans. These conditions increased the "squeeze of African populations" in general.[37] Moreover, the "apartheid regime was committed with total segregation of society—politically, socially, economically, educationally and culturally".[38]

In this atmosphere of high internal pressure in the Union of South Africa, certain circles fought to remove the constitutional barriers imposed against Africans, while pressure also came from abroad for a reform of the constitutional system in force, which limited the political participation of Africans and people of colour. They had limited political rights. In this atmosphere of political and economic struggle, a new generation of ANC leaders emerged, establishing bonds with the exterior. Moreover, the new leaders of ANC took part in meetings promoted by the mentors of pan-Africanism between 1945 and 1947.[39] Those were only diligences abroad among others that had already been carried out.

---

[37] Leonard Thompson (2014, 155) sees the time lapse from 1910 to 1948 as the "Era of Segregation". Besides, he thinks that the period of industrial growth of South Africa coincided with the period "when colonialism and segregation, reinforced by the racist assumption, prevailed in other places in Africa and also in many of Asia and the Caribbean, and racist ideas and practices were much extended in the United States".

[38] Alan Wieder, 2013, 61.

[39] Leonard Thompson, op. cit., 182.

Internally, however, there were more than evident inequalities between Africans, South Africans of British origin, and Afrikaners (Sampie Terreblanche, 2016).[40] But for them the "ethnic identity was more important than occupational and class differences". On this basis the National Party and other organisations of Afrikaner origin focused their efforts to deploy "Afrikaner cultural, economic, and political power".[41] Under that perspective, along with other dynamics, the National Party became, in 1943, the main force of parliamentary opposition. Five years later, in 1948, the National Party and the Afrikaner Party formed an electoral coalition,[42] which allowed winning the election and controlling political power in the Union of South Africa.[43] Having conquered power, the National Party reformulated the internal political scene and "removed traces of black participation in the central political system".[44] Besides, the National Party followed the trail of Afrikaner interests,[45] imposing ever grater obstacles to the circulation of Africans. Moreover, Alan Wieder (2013), when reviewing the present

---

[40] The historian Sampie Terreblanche, in his work *A History of Inequality in South Africa 1652–2002*, notes that "Few countries in the world are as renowned as South Africa for the sharp contrast between extravagant wealth and luxury on the one hand, and extreme poverty and destitution on the other. While, in the past, socio-economic inequality in South Africa had a racial character, the greatest inequality is now experienced within the African group. As far as the total population is concerned, inequalities have now gained an obvious class character" (2016, 29).

[41] Leonard Thompson, op. cit., 183.

[42] Nelson Mandela, about the 1948 election, said: "The biggest event for the country in [1948] was the general election—general only inasmuch as three million whites could participate, but not one of the thirteen million Africans. We discussed whether to hold a protest. The central issue was: did an election in which only whites took part have any relevance to Africans? The answer, as far as the ANC, was that we could not remain indifferent, albeit excluded from the process. We were excluded, but stakeholders: the defeat of the National Party was in our interest and in that of all Africans" (2006, 225).

[43] Leonard Thompson, 2014, 186.

[44] Idem, 187.

[45] According to David Welsh, "[I]n late 1950 the basic structure of apartheid was established" (2009, 67).

situation, stressed that the victory of the National Party in 1948 was synonymous with "the continuance of the racist state".[46]

With these results, Afrikaners imposed their view of life, and all was conditioned to their interests. Hence, the historic records state:

> The government meanwhile Afrikanerized every state institution, appointing Afrikaners to both senior and junior positions in the civil service, army, police, and state corporations. Medical and legal professional associations, too, came increasingly under Afrikaner control. The government also assisted Afrikaners to close the economic gap between themselves and English-speaking white South Africans.[47]

This set of measures taken by the Afrikaner government allowed whites to exert control and achieve supremacy. Given the hegemony of the National Party, they strengthened every racial and segregationist law.[48] In these conditions the term *apartheid*[49] turned "from political slogan into a drastic, systematic programme of social engineering",[50] thereby materialising the dream of many Afrikaners under the leadership of the National Party.

Once apartheid was implanted, other forces rose to counter it. Despite the nationalist view of the National Party and the repressive laws that led to society being policed to the extreme, religious groups,

---

[46] According to Alan Wieder, "South Africa was clearly a racist state prior to the election of the Nationalist Party in 1948 and the initiation of forty-five consecutive years of apartheid rule" (2013, 60).

[47] Leonard Thompson, op. cit., 188.

[48] David Welsh sees this moment, which began in 1948 and lasted until 1959, as the "entrenchment of the National Party in power and expansion of discrimination" (*The Rise and Fall of Apartheid*, 2009, 52).

[49] From a conceptual point of view, the founding father of apartheid, that is, its architect was Hendrik Frensch Verwoerd. Thus Henry Kenney (2016), in his work *Verwoerd Architect of Apartheid*, describes his origins and political career until he reached the leadership of the National Party (1958–66).

[50] Leonard Thompson, op. cit., 188.

university circles, student associations, women's associations, writers, actors, artists, intellectuals, academicians, industrialists, and others rose their voices against the practices of apartheid.

In the first two years of the 1950s, Albert Luthuli was elected chairman of the African National Congress (ANC).[51] In 1952, the African National Congress (ANC) and the Indian Congress of South Africa joined efforts in their struggle and launched a "passive resistance campaign". These two organisations, along with the Communist Party of South Africa, and the Congress of Democrats were all integrated in the Congress Alliance. This congress was a means of political concertation between them, especially when those political forces that wrote the *Freedom Charter* came together in 1955.[52] Political campaigns that those organisations promoted fit within the strategy of non-violence as a way of overthrowing the system of apartheid. Nevertheless, due to the internal struggle for leadership inside the ANC and the differences arising from different conceptions about ways of fighting against the oppressor, Robert Sobukwe and some co-religionists departed from the party and formed, in 1959, the Pan Africanist Congress (PAC). This political force, eager to accelerate the political struggle, deployed the youth to violent confrontation, directly facing the police authorities of apartheid.

The Sharpeville incident took place in the first quarter of 1960, in which sixty Africans were killed. Several voices rose from inside and outside to condemn it. Under internal pressure, the South African State imposed a state of emergency, arrested about 11,500 people, and banished the African National Congress (ANC) and the Pan Africanist Congress (PAC) from politics.[53] They included the South African Communist Party in those measures. Those political forces went underground, and

---

[51] Scott Couper (2012) describes the life and work of Albert Luthuli, who was an icon of the struggle for the liberation of the South African people against apartheid. He received the Nobel Prize for Peace for his political positions and the integrity of their options for non-violent struggle. See the work *Albert Luthuli Bound by Faith*.
[52] Alan Wieder, 2013. pp.88-89.
[53] David Welsh, 2009, p.73.

some of their members went into exile with the aim of divulging the struggle and harnessing support abroad.

The situation imposed by apartheid and non-violent action did not have the desired effects. Regime forces repressed many people and caused many casualties. In 1960, those responsible began to seek political alternatives that might actually work. All internal opposition forces were interested in resorting to armed violence because fifty years of non-violent action had elapsed without encouraging results. For that reason, the ANC, the Pan Africanist Congress, and the Africana Resistance Movement (formed by whites) began working together to accomplish that purpose. From the point of view of Nelson Mandela, armed struggle was desirable. He stated:

> That step was decisive. For fifty years ANC had faced non-violence as a basic principle, unquestionable and indisputable. From that moment ANC became a different organisation. We were entering a new path, filled with dangers, a path of organised violence whose results we did not know and could not guess.
>
> Our strategy was to carry out selective attacks against military facilities, energy centrals, telephone lines and transport connections; such targets would not only hinder the military effectiveness of the State as frighten the supporters of the National Party, scare off foreign capital and weaken the economy.[54]

Having conceived the armed struggle, ANC founded their armed organisation in July 1960. On 16 December 1960, the armed branch of ANC—Umkhonto we Sizwe—carried out its first sabotage actions.[55] Thereafter, Umkhonto we Sizwe announced in a public statement:

---

[54] Nelson Mandela, 2006, 292, 303.
[55] Hugh Macmillan, analysing the issue of armed struggle, stresses that "the passage to armed struggle had been discussed within ANC and SACP since early 1950, but

> Units of Umkhonto we Sizwe today carried out actions against premises of the Government, in particular those that are related with the Apartheid policy and racial discrimination.... Umkhonto we Sizwe shall pursue in its struggle for freedom and democracy with new methods, required to complement the actions of the established national liberation movements.[56]

One year after the onset of armed struggle, the National Party reached its target when "they obtained a majority in a referendum of white voters" in 1961.[57] This unprecedented victory gave a green light to the government of the Union of South Africa to transform the country into the Republic of South Africa. Consequently, the South African State became more independent from Britain. This fact was a victory because it took place thirteen years after the arrival in power of the National Party (1948–61). But the autonomy achieved by South Africa arose from forces both internal and external, mainly from the changes in British policies since the second half of the twentieth century. Robert Tombs (2015, 772) explains:

> The end of empire [British] then came quickly. There were general causes: the economic, political and psychological effects of two world wars both in European states and in their colonies; the Cold War and Soviet-backed anti-colonialism; American ambivalence; pressure from the UN and not least white settler extremism, which led South Africa to leave Commonwealth in 1961.[58]

---

that was only after the Sharpeville massacre and the removal of ANC in 1960, in which that was a step from the abstract discussion through action". (2014, 23)
[56] Nelson Mandela, 2006, 305.
[57] Leonard Thompson, 2014, 188.
[58] Roberts Tombs, 2015, 772. The Republic of South Africa appeared on 31 May 1961.

By this time, Nelson Mandela was already commanding the armed struggle, and sabotage operations had been used in several places.[59] But given that armed struggle implied more activities, Nelson Mandela secretly went abroad in 1962 to seek the support and solidarity of other peoples.[60] Because the first actions carried out by the armed branch of ANC were a major challenge to the authorities of South Africa, countermeasures were taken. The result was the arrest and trial of the leaders of ANC, including Mandela, Sisulu, and Govan Mbeki. In these conditions the underground activities gained traction, and more militants went into exile.[61] With this strike, the struggle saw its first setback. The armed struggle stagnated until 1964.

Meanwhile, in 1975, South Africa invaded Angola. And in 1976, the internal political scene of South Africa was marked by the Soweto massacre, which became known because of the brutality of the security forces against young students. The Black Consciousness Movement, led by Steve Biko, was the root of mobilization and guidance of that student revolt.[62]

---

[59] Nelson Mandela explains that "in the early hours of December 16th ... homemade bombs exploded in electric power centrals and government offices in Johannesburg, Port Elizabeth and Durban" (2006, 304-05).

[60] Idem, 307–29.

[61] Raymond Suttner led a social and historic study of the organisation of the underground activities of the African National Congress (ANC) and the South Africa Communist Party (SACP) during the period in question and described the structuration of those forces: "In underground organisation, conspiratorial methods rule. This is partly because the work tends to consist of the activities of small groups of people. The reconstruction of the ANC and SACP underground after Rivonia was designed in small-scale units. People worked on a 'need to know' basis: person X may have interacted with person Y on one activity, but Y ought not to have known that X also related to person Z in connection with other activities" (2008, 87).

[62] The view of Cristi van der Westhuizen about this movement is as follows: "In late 1960, Black Conscience had emerged as a powerful philosophy that totally covered the concept of black people as 'more than appendixes of white society'" (2007, 103). Meanwhile, Priscilla Jana says that "Steve Biko's BCM [Black Consciousness Movement] was a philosophy that helped us to walk tall and we would remain loyal to it always, but the ANC had mastered the politics.... Only the ANC could provide the firepower to achieve our goals" (2016, 90).

The War in Southern Africa

From this information we may deepen our strategic analysis of the Republic of South Africa. Internal precedent has to do with clashes between Africans, Afrikaners, and British, which began long ago and continued until the twentieth century. External precedent regards the involvement of the defence forces of the Union of South Africa in the theatres of war in Europe, Africa, the Middle East, and Asia during the two World Wars, and the invasion and occupation of Southwest Africa, as well as participation in the war in Korea.

Other external influences arise from its ancient condition of British dominion and external bonds that helped affirm internal culture. When the British Empire established the colonial territories of the Union of South Africa, New Zealand, Canada, and Australia as independent lands, this opened the way for cooperation with between them. Improved relations implied negotiation and compromise. From a military point of view, according to historian R. Dale, relations were based on five perspectives: trust between parties, military cooperation with the Commonwealth Empire, participation in military missions abroad, internal missions of the armed forces, and transfer of knowledge and military means.[63]

The Union of South Africa cooperated with the British Empire in military matters, which entailed training officers; transferring resources, technology, and professional capacities; requisition of capacities; support to the military edification; and development of institutions. With this the defence forces of Union of South Africa grew in miscellaneous ways, assimilating ideas, military theories, and strategic thought. In this sense the Union of South Africa and the British Empire cooperated during fifty years in matters of defence,[64] not counting the British input from the Industrial Revolution. Moreover, the British industrialised

---

[63] R. Dale reviewed *The South African Armed Forces and Their Link with the United Kingdom and the Commonwealth of Nations, 1910–1961* (1979, 1–3).

[64] Although South Africa became a republic on 31 May 1961 and withdrew from the Commonwealth, the truth is that it pondered the "military implications" of leaving that organisation. As such, it was interested in maintaining cooperation in certain aspects. See *Oorsic Oor Verdediging En Krygstuigproduksie Tydperk 1960 Tot 1970*, pages 9 and 10.

the Union of South Africa in the nineteenth century, which process proceeded with cooperation for another fifty years in the twentieth century until the emergence of the Republic of South Africa. In short, British support, especially investments, was economically significant. External investments continued in the 1960s and 1970s, which greatly strengthened the South African economy, despite some disinvestment by Britain and other countries.

Security challenges in South Africa arose from structuring the apartheid system and the series of problems that emerged from demonstrations, protests, and revolutionary sabotage. These were led by the three main internal opposition forces: the African National Congress (ANC), the Pan Africanist Congress (PAC), and the Communist Party of South Africa (SACP).[65] Internal revolutionary forces maintained bonds with political forces of independent African states and other progressive forces that vehemently condemned colonialism and apartheid.

Some countries had achieved national independence: Tanzania, Zambia, Botswana, and Lesotho. In some colonies armed struggle had begun, such as Angola in 1961, Mozambique in 1964,[66] and Rhodesia in 1965.[67] In 1966, SWAPO began its guerrilla activity in the Caprivi

---

[65] Armed action by these forces since December 1961 stagnated in 1964, when many of their leaders were arrested while others were abroad, creating conditions to pursue the fight.

[66] War in Mozambique began in 1964. As Francisco Proença Garcia explains: "It is the actions of August 21st and 24th 1964, carried out by the independentist movements MANU and UDENAMO, in Cabo Delgado, which trigger violent action. FRELIMO initiated, almost simultaneously, its guerrilla operations in the district of Niassa with the attack on the secretary of the administrative outpost of Còbue, on September 24th, and in the province of Cabo Delgado with the attack on the Chai outpost, on the night from the 24th to the 25th of that month." (*História de Portugal Guerras e Campanhas Militares a Gerra de Moçambique 1964, 1974*, 2010, 38)

[67] Pauis Moorcraft and Peter Mclaughlin (2008) report the war of Rhodesia within the context of the military history of Zimbabwe. In the same line of thought, Joseph Mtisi, Munyaradzi Nyakudya, and Teresa Barnes (2014) also report the war of Rhodesia between 1965 and 1980.

The War in Southern Africa

Strip of Southwest Africa.[68] Hence, African nationalism was gaining ever more terrain in Southern Africa, which forced political and military cooperation between South Africa, Portugal, and Rhodesia and establishment of common strategies against those nationalist forces. Externally also, several organisations condemned apartheid and colonialism, including the United Nations (UN) and the Organisation of African Unity (OAU), and organisations that stood for human rights, equality, and social justice. South Africa was also in a condition of isolation being under several sanctions and many restrictions, which increased internal and external pressure.

The strategic conception of South Africa was built on the vision and will of the National Party. The total national strategy of South Africa is expressed in the history of the country since the National Party conquered and consolidated political power. Therefore the guiding lines of the total national strategy are expressed in official documents produced by the South African state itself, namely: white papers on defence.[69] According to the *White Paper on Defence* of the period from 1960 to 1970,[70] South African perception was that the worldwide political atmosphere of 1960 was unstable, and that would have implications on internal peace and security. Furthermore, for them peace between East and West was based on "fear of nuclear war". They also thought that withdrawal from West Africa had caused "quick deterioration of the position of whites in Southern Africa while Communism [exerted] ever more influence in the rest of Africa". According to them, the "African continent would play a

---

[68] Within the struggle for the liberation of Namibia, in "1964–65 the first militants returned as guerrilla warriors trained to organise rural bases to train local populations. And in October of that year the Caprivi African National Union (CANU) associated with SWAPO, closing a regional chasm, and widened the base of popular support to an area then isolated.... The first military encounter took place on August 26th, when SWAPO fighters from the Omgulumbashe base, in Ovamboland, clashed with South African troops." (*Nasce Uma Nação: A Luta de Libertação da Namíbia*, Information and Publicity Department, Namibia SWAPO, 1985, 195)

[69] Although that is the case, it is also true that not all white papers on defence mirror the vision of national strategy, but they enhance many more aspects of military defence of South Africa.

[70] Titled *Oorsic Oor Verdediging En Krygstuigproduksie Tydperk 1960 Tot 1970*.

key role in the traditional strategy for the Soviets and an attack would focus on the white Governments of Southern Africa."[71] Meanwhile, in 1961, as we saw, the Union of South Africa became the Republic of South Africa.

This change generated different reactions around the world, all against the birth of the Republic of South Africa. That was another moment that strengthened the strategic thought and vision of South Africa because several states were not pleased with the emergence of a white republic in Southern Africa. Hence an arms embargo was proposed to the United Nations and Western countries against South Africa on 18 June 1964. On 17 November the British government imposed an "arms boycott" on South Africa, which embarrassed its defence department and revealed its fragilities.[72] Facing this situation, the strategy was to abandon dependence and create national capacities. First, to "establish a Weapons Council" with specific tasks; to explore its "own scientific possibilities and industrial capacities" given the continuous "economic growth of the Republic"; to use the "qualities of scientists"; to establish a "Corporation for Production and Development of Weapons (ARMCOR)"; to create "self-sufficiency in the medical services of South Africa", etc.,[73] all to guarantee its own national capacities.

In the White Paper on Defence 1964–1965, White Paper on Defence 1965–67, White Paper on Defence and Armament Production 1969, and White Paper on Defence and Armament Production 1973, they made comments aimed at reinforcing the defence capacities due to "non-conventional threats that existed in the form of terrorism" and considering "the possibility of a conventional attack". They also mentioned that "the non-conventional threat had increased" from the territories of Rhodesia, Angola, and Mozambique.[74] Besides, based on

---

[71] *Idem*, 5.
[72] *Idem*, 10.
[73] *Idem*, 11–14.
[74] *White Paper on Defence and Armament Production 1973*, 4.

contrary strategies, they identified threats to the Republic of South Africa, such as:

efforts to isolate the Republic of South Africa from the rest of the world community, for example by the imposition of economic boycotts; by persistent unfavourable propaganda, boycotts; and demonstrations in the spheres of sport and art, even in those of science and culture;

the prevention of all armament sales to the Republic of South Africa;

the creation of internal disturbances to disrupt law and order;

the support and encouragement of terrorism against the Republic of South Africa;

the creation of real and fictitious situations that could be exploited to persuade the UN to declare that these were a threat to world peace;

efforts to persuade the Western powers to approve and support the UN in a possible intervention by force.[75]

To this point there is no clear exposition about the total national strategy of South Africa. The understanding that one can draw concerns the need to create national capacities to face the different threats, especially those of a military nature. But in the *White Paper on Defence and Armament Production of 1975*, the head of government, P. W. Botha, highlighted the value of total strategy as a sum of political, economic, diplomatic, and military activities aimed at achieving the political aims of the state.[76] Botha's warning took into consideration developments in Angola and Mozambique in the scope of their independences. Hence, in October 1975, South Africans enacted their plan and invaded Angola. But South African military intervention was a failure. Due to

---

[75] *Idem*, 5.
[76] *White Paper on Defence and Armament Production 1975*, 3.

that failure, and foreseeing other scenarios from the point of view of national security, Botha spoke about the value of "total effort against total onslaught" during a speech in an inaugural class before students of the University of Stellenbosch in 1976.[77]

The Guiding Lines of the Total National Strategy

In the prevailing situation in Southern Africa, the South African government published the *White Paper on Defence 1977*, exposing its total national strategy from an interdepartmental perspective.[78] The *White Paper on Defence 1977*, of the mandate of P. W. Botha, highlights:

The National Security Situation[79]

12. South Africa was far from the epicentre of world events and played virtually no parts of the world balance of power. However, developments in Africa and elsewhere have today thrust the Republic of South Africa against its will into the foreground, where the attainment of the National Security Aims is directly affected by occurrences and trends of thought beyond our borders.

13. World peace rests mainly upon the balance of military might between the western democracies and Marxist powers and it is this very balance which is the foundation of a stable international order. Paradoxically, however, the state of international stability, based largely on the essential nuclear balance between the two super powers, lends itself in instability at lower levels, and Southern Africa is one of the many victims of this regional instability.

14. During the two years since the 1975 White Paper was Tabled in the Senate and the House of Assembly, considerable changes have taken place in the world, and particularly in the southern region of Africa.

---

[77] *Paratus*, March 1976, 13.
[78] *White Paper on Defence 1977*, 4–5.
[79] Emphasis added.

a. <u>Southern Africa</u>. The most significant occurrences were in Mozambique and Angola, which gained independence on 25 June and 11 November 1975 respectively. With the establishment of minority governments in these territories, it became apparent that stability in Mozambique and Angola would not be achieved for a long time to come. Both countries are faced with serious economic crises and they have been obliged to launch comprehensive programmes for political, social and military consolidation. Whilst independence came comparatively peacefully to Mozambique, the circumstances in Angola were quite different and had a considerable effect on the RSA's security interests. In both cases propaganda campaigns against the stable governments in Southern Africa were intensified.

b. <u>RSA Involvement in Angola</u>. In the first place it was necessary for the RSA to intervene on a limited scale in Angola to safeguard her security interests. South Africa responded to a call from the works on the Calueque-Ruacana scheme to protect them in the situation which had resulted from the Portuguese withdrawal and the absence of any form of governmental authority in that area. This military intervention was then extended in order to deflect the effects of the Angolan civil war from the northern border of South-West Africa and inhibit SWAPO efforts to capitalise on the unstable situation in the southern region of Angola. The other aspect where military forces were involved concerned the protection and administration of civil war refugees. Despite the anti-South African propaganda unleashed in an effort to discredit the South African forces in Angola, factual evidence makes it quite clear that these forces gave an excellent account of themselves in their contact with opposing forces, including the Cuban troops assisting the MPLA. Regrettably our forces suffered some casualties, but these were limited in relation to the overall results achieved.

c. Soviet/Cuban Intervention in Angola. The other impact of events in Angola on the RSA's security interests was more complex and will probably have far-reaching consequences in long run. This refers to the Soviet and Cuban intervention in the civil war with the aim of bringing to power a government which would be well-disposed towards the Marxist cause. This is a clear indication of Soviet imperialism which will confront Africa in the future. One can justifiably say that there is a Soviet shadow over parts of Africa.

d. Threat to the RSA. The threat to the Republic of South Africa has not changed in form and substance since the SA Defence Force Military Strategy was outlined in the 1973 and 1975 White Papers. The occurrences in Africa and elsewhere have, however, led to an increase in the tempo of developments and this has brought the threats nearer in time.

e. The Present National Security Situation. The relative proximity of Soviet influence and military aid has had its effect on terrorist activities against the northern areas of South-West Africa and on the internal situation of our country. The general trend of events following the coup in Portugal in April 1974 has led to a state of decreased stability in areas to the north of the RSA.

f. Increased Tempo of Developments. With the increased tempo of developments in Southern Africa and in the international sphere, the factors which affect the RSA's total national strategy, its policies, force levels and required defence expenditure have been profoundly influenced. Adaptations must continually be made in order to keep the degree of readiness in balance with the various threats.

Factors Which Influence the Total National Strategy

17. There are many factors which influence the formulation of the total national strategy of the RSA. The decisive and most determinative factors are however the strategy of the RSA's enemies and the RSA's national aims, objectives and policies.

18. The Strategy, Policies and Aims of the RSA's Enemies.

The War in Southern Africa

These can be summarised:

a. The expansion of Marxism by fomenting revolution in Southern Africa.
b. The overthrow of the white regimes in Southern Africa so that the militant Africa bloc can realise its aspirations with regards to the distraction of so-called colonialism and racialism and the establishment of Pan-Africanism. In its desire to destroy alleged racism, the Arab Bloc in its hostile actions as far as this serves its own purpose.
c. The striving after an indirect strategy in order to unleash revolutionary warfare in Southern Africa and, by means isolation, to force the RSA to change its domestic policy in favour of Pan-Africanism.

19. African states do not possess the ability to successfully initiate aggression against the RSA, but some African countries are supported by a super power with the ability to simultaneously wage integrated revolutionary and conventional warfare.

20. The RSA's National Aims. In contrast the national aims of the RSA as set out in the preamble to the Constitution are:

a. To stand united: to strive for the ideal of co-existence of all peoples in South Africa.
b. To maintain law and order in the RSA: and thereby to secure the authority of the government and its institutions.
c. To safeguard the inviolability and freedom of the RSA.
d. To further the contentment and spiritual and material welfare of all and to strive for world peace in association with all peace-loving nations.

21. The National Objectives. In order to realise these aims the state has as its goal the continued existence of the RSA and all its people by:

a. the orderly development and maintenance of the body politic;

b. the preservation of the identity, dignity, the right to self-determination and the integrity of all population groups;
c. the identification, prevention and countering of revolution, subversion and any other form of unconstitutional action;
d. the maintenance of a sound balance of military power in relation to neighbouring states and other states in Southern Africa;
e. aiming for the greatest possible measure of economic and social development, and the maximum self-sufficiency;
f. the creation of friendly relationships and political and economic cooperation with the states of Southern Africa;
g. planning total national strategy at government level for co-ordinated action between all government departments, government institutions and other authorities to counter the multi-dimensional onslaught against the RSA in the ideological, military, economic, social, psychological, cultural, political and diplomatic fields.

22. National Policies. National policies to achieve specific aims and objectives are of cardinal importance:

a. Internal. The internal policy is based mainly on the question of human relationships in a plural society:
   i. to follow a policy of independent development of all population groups—the cornerstone of internal relations;
   ii. to lead the homelands of the RSA to self-determination and independence;
   iii. to further Coloured and Indian interests by the creation of their own government bodies and, by the establishment of constitutional machinery, to serve matters and actions of communal interest;
   iv. to acknowledge and to maintain the dignity of the population groups in the RSA;
   v. to counter with all our might Marxism or any other form of revolutionary action by any group or movement.

b. South-West Africa. To assist the inhabitants and the various populations groups of SWA to shape their own political future and to prevent any external interference in any sphere in that territory.

c. External. The foreign policy of the RSA is based on its internal policy. According the RSA endeavours:

   i. through dialogue and assistance, from a position of strength, to normalise relationship, whenever possible, with all countries in Africa, particularly those in Southern Africa;
   ii. to achieve understanding by governments and citizens of other countries of the RSA's internal policies and the western humanistic tradition upon which they are based;
   iii. to emphasize the strategic importance of the R.S.A., the danger of Marxist infiltration and the extent of the thread of revolutionary take-over in Southern Africa in order to prevent, through Western diplomatic action, the build-up of Marxist influence and military power in neighbouring states.[80]

To formulate the present total national strategy of the Republic of South Africa, they considered the political, diplomatic, economic, and military aspects, as well as the international political atmosphere and its impact on the internal situation. They also valued circumstances in Africa and Southern Africa in particular, especially the situations prevailing in Angola and Mozambique. They also identified the threats and their nature, as well as the real situation regarding South Africa's security. Thereafter they set targets and national political aims and established guidelines for domestic and foreign policy.

We have revealed some elements of the total national strategy of South Africa. Let us, nevertheless, proceed with the analysis of other components of the total national strategy. One must thus review foreign policy, defence policy, strategic doctrine, military policy, and the issue of use of force by the state.

---

[80] See *White Paper on Defence 1977*, 6-9.

CHAPTER 2

The Two Fundamental Strategies

This chapter describes the foreign policy of this period in all its nuances and explains aspects regarding defence policy, military policy, and strategic doctrines.

The External Political Strategy

The foreign policy of South Africa emanated from of its domestic policy, as is the case with the different states. But the grounds of foreign policy were patent in the political history of the country. From a historic point of view, the initial milestone of that policy has to do with the advent and evolution of the Union of South Africa during the first quarter of the twentieth century. In 1926, however, the Union of South Africa found the golden opportunity to establish and develop an autonomous foreign policy, when the territories that were British dominions signed the *Balfour Declaration* together with Britain. This declaration gave powers to said territories to conceive their internal and external policies despite their bonds to the Commonwealth. Hence, the territories became independent politically and diplomatically. In other words, the foreign policy of the Union of South Africa gained traction after the signature of the *Balfour Declaration* in 1926.

But when the Union of South Africa conquered that autonomy, from the foreign policy perspective, the Afrikaner communities and their nationalist parties were fighting for political domination. At the time,

Afrikaner nationalism was marching at full steam. The Afrikaner feat took place in 1948, the reference date of full domination by Afrikaner nationalists. From that point the National Party dictated domestic policy and diplomatic guidelines in conformity with the project of Afrikaner nationalists. With the advent of the Republic of South Africa, they carried on in the same trail. Nevertheless, let us look at other features of foreign policy.

Given that the instruments that allow implementing foreign policy decisions may be diplomatic, economic, psychological, and military, the choice fell on diplomacy, albeit articulated with the military instrument. The *diplomacy of defiance* was conceived out of this. That diplomatic line centred efforts to keep the apartheid system in the country and "win friends and repel enemies".[81] The meaning thereby expressed arises from the fact that "war and diplomacy are the main instruments of domestic policy and foreign policy". Besides, what was at sake were relations between states that were sovereign entities.[82] *Preventative* diplomacy was not at the core of the diplomacy of defiance. It was utterly *coercive* diplomacy; its mainstay was force. Coercive diplomacy brings forth security and national interests. "[O]ne may say that politically it is the ability (will and resources) to put force at the service of diplomacy, instead of placing diplomacy at the service of force." (Maria Regina Mongiardin, 2007, 23)[83]

The diplomacy of defiance stood long but was executed according to the differing visions of leaders of the National Party that led the country from 1948 to 1989. The leaders of the National Party—D. F. Malan (1948–54), J. G. Strijdom (1954–58), Hendrik Verwoerd (1958–66), John Voster (1966–77) and P. W. Botha (1978–89)—left their personal marks on foreign policy and even on the diplomatic action of the country. Therefore, in their mandates, diplomatic actions varied, but the force element was a preferential mark. But an analysis of foreign policy

---

[81] John Siko, 2014, 17.
[82] See *Diplomacy and Strategy: Patterns in the Diplomacy of Black Southern African States,* in *ISSP Strategic Review*, March 1981, p. 2 Besides, A. du Plessis stresses that there are "inverse relationship trends between diplomacy and military means".
[83] *Diplomacia*, 2007.

The War in Southern Africa

extends to 1989 only because thereafter there were changes introduced by F. W. de Klerk, the reformist leader of the National Party.

From 1948 to 1958, foreign policy was based on the conception of a *balancing act*. The Union of South Africa established relations with the Western world. It faced external pressure; supported the efforts of the North Atlantic Treaty Organisation (NATO) in the Southern Hemisphere; tried to control the border territories that were protectorates of Britain (Swaziland, Botswana, and Lesotho); and made an approximation to the first African independent states in the 1950s—Ghana and others—without any success.[84] But D. F. Malan, during his term as prime minister, implemented several segregationist and racist measures and launched offensive action against the *defiance campaign* triggered by the internal political forces that fought the apartheid. Given that the internal situation was challenged, he warned the world to not interfere "in South Africa's domestic affairs".[85] And he felt "motivated by the considerations of realpolitik".[86] He was a relentless defender of political realism. However, due to political contradictions within the National Party, D. F. Malan resigned. J. G. Strijdom, his arch-rival inside the party, took his office on 30 November 1954.

J. G. Strijdom led the National Party for four years.[87] In 1958, meanwhile, Hendrik Verwoerd came to power and became leader of the National Party. This political leader, imbued with the ideas of apartheid and the need for greater mobility, inflicted the course of foreign policy in the country. He conceived the foreign policy of the Union of South Africa in view of *politics of withdrawal*. This explains the political facts concerning the emergence of the Republic of South Africa in 1960 and its withdrawal from the Commonwealth. He withdrew the country from this organisation and, contrary to expectations, the economy grew.

---

[84] John Siko, 2014.
[85] Lindie Koorts, 2014, 380. "Nelson Mandela contributed as volunteer-in-chief to the Defiance Campaign in 1952, in which volunteers in the ANC and allied organisations openly defied apartheid laws and asked government for African representation on all levels of government." See Hermann Giliomee, 2012, 79.
[86] Idem, 383.
[87] J. L. Basson, 1980, 604.

Moreover, "the first years of the Republic of South Africa were times of spectacular economic expansion" and this "also made it invulnerable to external attacks".[88]

Because of the intransigence of Hendrik Verwoerd on the internal front, relations between South Africa and the United Nations worsened and became grey after the Sharpeville massacre of 1960. Pressure against South Africa increased due to the impact of internal events in the international arena. That led the United Nations to impose a trade and diplomatic boycott on South Africa and to decree a weapons embargo against the country. In this situation, and facing pressure from progressive countries, the South African leader, following the idea of politics of withdrawal, proceeded with his internal and external projects. Furthermore, he strengthened bonds of friendship with the Western world and tried to establish economic bonds with neighbouring African countries. As for recently independent African countries, he agreed with their independences as he wished the same for certain land parcels (*homelands*) within South Africa. But he thought that they were happening speedily.[89]

Meanwhile, on 3 December 3 1966, Hendrik Verwoerd was murdered.[90] With the death of this prime minister, deemed the architect and propeller of apartheid, John Voster reached power.[91]

John Voster (1966–77) led foreign policy based on the perspective of *uphill struggle for engagement.* This formulation of foreign policy was caused by pressure from the United Nations, African countries, and Eastern Europe. His priorities included establishing diplomatic

---

[88] Henry Kenny, 2016, 285.
[89] Henry Kenney, 2016, 284.
[90] Henry Kenney, in his work *Verwoerd Architect of Apartheid*, analysed the career of this leader of the National Party in the field of foreign policy as a "maker of foreign policy", highlighting: "As conductor of foreign policy Verwoerd displayed exceptional abilities. His supreme aim was the same as at home: preservation of the white man's position in South Africa. In principle, he was as little prepared to make concessions in his dealing with the outside world as in the enforcement of apartheid in the Republic itself. The safety of the white man was never negotiable" (298).
[91] According to Hermann Giliomee, "Verwoerd's final five years represented the apogee of the apartheid system" (2012, 85).

bonds in the African continent, incrementing relations with the United States of America and Western Europe, and creating economic and diplomatic bonds with other parts of the world.[92] John Voster, in his diplomatic efforts, acted under the pressure of members of the Afrikaner community that "recognised the danger of international isolation" of South Africa.[93]

To mitigate isolation within the African continent, the initiatives of John Voster allowed establishing political and economic bonds with African countries such as Malawi, Ivory Coast, Senegal, Gabon, Madagascar, and Central African Republic. But in Liberia, Ghana, and Kenya, he was unlucky as these countries rejected South African advances. He visited some African countries and spoke to their leaders (Leabua Jonathan, Hastings Banda, Seretse Khama, and Kenneth Kaunda).[94] He thought that peace in the region of South Africa would be the key factor for development, and he believed that one should work for peace and normalising relations. In his view, this was the "first aim".[95]

John Voster carried on. In the mid-1960s he materialised the idea of creating a Southern Atlantic Pact between the navies of South Africa, Brazil, and Argentina, but everything failed because of condemnations of apartheid.[96] During the 1970s John Voster strengthened relations with NATO and created diplomatic bonds with the dictatorships of Latin America: Brazil, Argentina, Paraguay, Uruguay, and Chile. Meanwhile, he pursued efforts with other countries—Taiwan, Iran and Israel—with which economic and military cooperation yielded results and helped both internal security and the operation of the national economy.

---

[92] John Siko, 2014, 20.
[93] Idem, 20. As this author stated: "Voster engaged in a continent-wide charm offensive that primarily used economic incentives to try to win political support in African capitals" (21).
[94] John d'Oliveira, 1977, 250–52.
[95] Idem, 250.
[96] Pieter Wolvaardt, 1999.

In 1970, prime minister John Voster visited Portugal, where he discussed certain situations with Marcelo Caetano. When he returned to South Africa, he said:

> When it came to the question of independence for Portuguese territories like Mozambique and Angola, I never actually suggested that Caetano should give them independence. However at that stage Caetano was greatly perturbed about our intention of giving self-government to Owambo because he believed that it ran contrary to his own concept of what should happen in Angola and Mozambique. You must not forget that Portugal, a small European country, set great store by these two vast tracts of African land. When it came to the future of Portugal in Africa, I think that, in my own mind, the writing was already on the wall. But it is like a very sick man. You know he his sick and you are almost certain that he is going to die, it always seems to take you by surprise. And this is how the Spinola coup and the subsequent events in Portugal and its African provinces affected me. This despite the fact that it had gradually dawned on me that the longer the wars in both Mozambique and Angola carried on, the worse the situations in those territories would become. This fed into my thinking and it naturally affected my planning and policies. All this meant that I knew I would have to live with independent and possibly even hostile states on my borders. That is why South Africa adopted the attitude that she was not interested in who formed a government or in what kind of a government it was. She was only interested that it should be a good government.[97]

---

[97] John d'Oliveira, 1977, 253-54.

John Voster's words are clear. South Africa was aware of the critical situation that Portugal was in and knew what types of internal developments could take place. And it knew that this would have significant impact on the Portuguese overseas territories and their safety. Therefore, South Africa was alert and ready to adjust its plans and policies so that this would not jeopardise its interests. In the mid-1970s, nevertheless, changes happened in Portugal. Because of this, the South Africa defence forces intervened in Angola. One year later, South Africa was banished from the United Nations.

The Soweto massacre took place in the following year (1976), followed by the death of activist Steve Biko. These internal events and the regional problems much worsened the condition of a pariah state. Moreover, in 1977 the United Nations imposed, a weapons embargo on the country to contain its impulses. Internally, however, John Voster was involved in a scandal that shook his condition as a political leader. P. W. Botha took his place.

P. W. Botha (1978–89) inaugurated a new era in South African diplomacy. According to John Siko, the ascension of Botha to the office of prime minister favoured the emergence of "new muscularity … [in] foreign engagement".[98] He favoured military interventions in regional conflicts and encouraged a greater programme of nuclear development. Hence the defence and security forces gained a central role and a "predominant position in the formulation of foreign policy". Nevertheless, Botha also manipulated political and economic positions in the scope of Southern Africa.[99] But he failed in his policy of approximation because the other countries in the region were already congregated to face South

---

[98] John Siko, 2014, 23.

[99] T. Malan (1983) says that the idea arose from academicians and experts given the situation in Africa. Hence in 1979, South Africa proposed the establishment of a Constellation de States of Southern Africa (CONSAS). This organisation would have the aim of dealing with economic cooperation and "could eventually develop common approaches in the fields of politics and security" (In *New Dimensions in Southern African Economic Relationships*, 2–20).

Africa.[100] They had already formed the Southern African Development Coordination Conference (SADCC).

But in 1984, P. W. Botha and Samora Machel signed the Nkomati Agreement with the aim of containing military action between the two countries and guaranteeing security to their citizens. Likewise with the aim of containing the expansion of communism in Southern Africa, Botha tried to get closer to the Soviet Union, seeking an understanding.[101]

On the other hand, the situation being critical inside South Africa, he made efforts in 1985 to free Nelson Mandela, who refused the proposal from the counterparty.[102] Despite every action launched by Botha, the "international isolation of South Africa continued rapidly".[103] The internal situation at the time was unsustainable due to the People's War. This war began in 1984, intensified in 1985, and continued into following years.[104] The country faced a critical situation, one that forced Botha to declare a state of national emergency. During his mandate, Botha maintained his foreign policy, continuously granting an upper place to the defence and security forces. He remained adamant in his foreign policy and in its diplomatic practices and actions to the end of his consulate because they were guided by the Total Onslaught ideology.[105]

Still reflecting on the foreign policy and diplomatic strategies of South Africa, as they represented an important link from the point of view of the national security strategy, one must introduce other considerations. South African foreign policy faced international denial, which much hindered its aims of being a striking policy in defence of the national interests of South Africa. Despite international denial, the South African State handled its foreign policy on the basis of opportunities that Botha created and others that were provided

---

[100]
[101] Hermann Giliomee, 2012, 176.
[102] Idem, 187.
[103] Idem, 190.
[104] Anthea Jeffery, 2009, 41–85.
[105] Robert Schire and Daniel Silke, 1997.

by other states due to economic interests and gains for economic groups belonging to those spaces. Certain states isolated South Africa, but for others it was an ally of strategic and economic importance. Reflect on the relations between the United States of America and South Africa. US foreign policy regarding South Africa went through stages and progressed in conformity with the policies of changing US administrations. An explanation of this matter is in the work *U. S. Foreign Policy Towards Apartheid South Africa, 1948–1994 Conflict of Interests* by Alex Thomson. In the second half of the twentieth century, the African continent was not a "priority for US foreign policy".[106] The sole priority of US foreign policy in the African continent was its relationship with South Africa. They chose South Africa as a strategic partner and maintained the alliance, built on mutual interests.

In practice, relations between the United States of America and South Africa were structured upon the strategic value of this country in containing the advance of communism in Southern Africa and upon reciprocal economic benefits. Privileged relations between the parties had to do with considerable stocks of strategic minerals in this African country and assets and services that it imported from the US, which helped develop the economy of this country.

The US also made heavy investments in the South African economy. They also depended greatly on its strategic minerals.[107] The Americans tried to keep a balanced relationship with their counterparty to obtain "strategic benefits" from the other side of the Atlantic. Strategic issues and economic interests strengthened relations between the two countries. This relationship lasted throughout the second half of the twentieth century. Nevertheless, inside the United States of America and its administrations, voices had long ago risen to condemn the practices of the apartheid regime.

---

[106] Alex Thomson, 2008, 1.
[107] Ibidem, 8. Moreover, according to this author, "the level of dependence of the United States and its allies on this one country for [chromium, manganese, platinum and vanadium] minerals had strategic implications".

In general, the establishment and maintenance of relations with South Africa was primordial for these Western states. As such the West, mainly the United States of America and Britain, tried to preserve relations with South Africa, despite the prevailing criticism in several Western circles and sanctions imposed by the United Nations. Meanwhile, relations with those Western countries recorded highs and lows. At a certain time, those relations fell to very low levels that worsened the condition of the isolated country. At the same time, this situation had significant impact on its internal politics and the national security strategy.

Note that the state was a weakened *player* in the context of international relations, despite its military, economic, and scientific prowess. This analysis gains traction with the comments made by D. J. Geldenhuys in an opinion text titled "The International Isolation of South Africa".[108] This paper focuses on the international isolation of South Africa compared with Chile, Israel, and Taiwan, countries that also had situations of isolation in the same period. It highlights that the isolation of South Africa could be identified with the use of "thirty indicators" grouped into "four areas of isolation", namely: "diplomatic, economic, military and sociocultural".[109] Due to the realities configured, for Geldenhuys, South Africa was a state with a "pariah image".

Geldenhuys mentioned that the "Republic [of South Africa was] one of the most isolated States in the world […] [There was], in other words, a causal relation between Apartheid and international ostracism. But it is also true that isolationism had deeper roots because 'elements of voluntary isolation' [were] patent in South African foreign relations since 1948".[110] Specifically, when the National Party reached power.

---

[108] See *Strategic Review for Southern Africa*, Vol XI No 2, November 1989.
[109] D. J. Geldenhuys, 1989, 39.
[110] Idem, 40. According to this author, "[the] process of pariahsation has extended beyond the South African government: White South Africans, more specifically Afrikaners, have become a pariah people. There is an international stereotype that depicts Afrikaners in particular as a uniquely evil people…. Probably the vast majority of foreign states do not acknowledge the South African government's right to rule and to represent the people of the country." Idem, 43.

The internal political developments that took place from 1948 to 1960 and thereafter, under the National Party, reinforced that "voluntary isolation" and created conditions for international isolation of the country.

To illustrate the isolation of South Africa, D. J. Geldenhuys mentioned the "indicators of economic isolation". They covered foreign trade, commercial representations, foreign investment, loans, and transfer of technologies. As he wrote, "at least 100 countries officially limited business with South Africa and more than 90 percent of export goods from the Republic was affected by foreign restrictions".[111] Still, South Africa faced a disinvestment campaign involving economic and religious entities.

In these conditions, and according to information from the US institution Investor Responsibility Research Center, seven US corporations abandoned South Africa in 1984, 38 in 1985 and 48 in 1986. In mid-1988, more than 160 US firms left, more than one third of the total number [operating] in South Africa in 1984. Total US investment total [in the Republic of South Africa] reached 2.4 billion dollars in 1982, in 1987 it fell to less than 1 billion dollars. Between January 1984 and June 1988, some 115 non-US multinationals also disinvested in South Africa, 49 of which were British.[112]

The trade restrictions were a fact that extended to the transfer of technologies. In this field, nuclear and computation technologies were the most affected. Moreover, the United States of America, Sweden, and the European community forbade collaboration with South Africa in the nuclear sector. Military isolation was also notorious and affected all areas.[113] As D. J. Geldenhuys stressed: "one can reasonably conclude that

---

[111] Idem, 49.
[112] D. J. Geldenhuys, 1989, 50–51.
[113] South African economy in the early 1980s (1980–81) was growing 5 per cent to 7 per cent yearly. It then went into "virtual stagnation", despite important business partnerships since 1983. In 1985 it again recorded "real negative growth". In 1986, the economy grew less than 1 per cent, then 2.1 per cent in 1987 and 3.2 per cent in 1988. However, export products recorded a decline between 1986 and 1987. Given the critical situation of the country's economy, foreigners withdrew their capital, and

no other economy is subject, today, to the huge international political pressure and punishment placed on South Africa".[114] In the final part of his op-ed, Geldenhuys, head of the political science department of the Rand Afrikaans University of Johannesburg in the late 1980s, said:

> South Africa's international ostracism is extensive, covering all four major areas identified. In each of the economic, military and socio-cultural spheres, South Africa is on the whole far more isolated than Israel, Chile or Taiwan. [...]. A second special feature is that South Africa's international ostracism is combined with more widespread and intense international pressure and punishment than is experienced by any of the other three states. South Africa, it can be said, faces a unique combination of isolation and intervention.[115]

Lastly, Geldenhuys said: "In South Africa's case, a lifting of isolation would require that the basic cause of its ostracism—Apartheid—should finish."[116]

Following these interrogations, one may legitimately make others. In the context of the domestic political atmosphere of South Africa in the 1980s, was it possible to make changes in foreign policy?

Changes in the field of foreign policy would be possible only if internal political reform was implemented. Moreover, academician G. C. Olivier, in a reflection made in 1981 titled *Strategy and Tactics for Change in South Africa*, defended internal reform from a social and political point of view and believed that this was a transversal task. At the same time, reform constituted a complex task within South African

---

South Africa sustained heavy losses in its external reserves. "The economic problem of stagnation of the South African economy arose from the interaction of economic and political factors". See G. L. de Wet, in *Strategic Planning and the South African Economic Situation*, 1989, 20–27.

[114] Idem, 53.
[115] Idem, 58–59.
[116] D. J. Geldenhuys, 1989, 59.

society due to its specificities. Although there was a wish for reform, the truth is that challenges remained that represented obstacles to change.

Still (according to this scholar), the most expressive impediment in the path to reform was the very "Afrikaner establishment" and its communities. In other words, there was a struggle "between progressive and conservative Afrikaner elements about desirable reform and its contents".[117]

Another obstacle to reform that arose consisted of the model of society to be created, as some were interested in a model of "decentralised confederate paradigm" and others in a model of "centralised unitary paradigm". Whites wanted a "decentralised system" and non-whites (blacks) were interested in a "mostly centralised system."[118]

Deep down what was at stake was reforming the "traditional paradigm" based on "white domination" and a base of separate development.[119] The struggle was fought between preservation of the status quo and against it. "Reform in our times became an imperative for several reasons: the monopoly and nature of the system of white domination invokes dangerous reactions that increase non-white aspirations, polarisation along racial lines and the external reaction to the so-called Apartheid system."[120]

It is necessary to incorporate other opinions in pursuing the reflection about foreign policy and change. Roger D. Spegele and Colin Vale, in a study about theoretical and practical implications of change in South Africa's foreign policy, stress that the "connection between the foreign relations of South Africa and its internal dilemmas had seldom been examined or exposed in South African politics. It is certainly well known that the difficult state of South African relations with the African Continent, the West and the Third World caused discomfort, high costs and humiliations in the past and will produce more, probably exacerbated, in the future".[121] The prevailing framework

---

[117] G. C. Oilvier, 1983, 383.
[118] Idem.
[119] Idem, 385.
[120] G. C. Olivier, 382.
[121] Roger D. Spegele and Colin Vale, 1983, 426.

required treatment adequate to the internal crisis. Hence, they carried on until change arose.

On this discussion of the external political strategy of South Africa, only a few ideas remain to review. The geopolitics of war dominated foreign policy during the apartheid era (1948–89). They also made of foreign policy "a virtual extension and exportation of the domestic policy of Apartheid", with all associated elements arising from the Cold War.[122] The People's Republic of Angola confronted the diplomatic policies of John Voster and P. W. Botha. But "historically South Africa was vulnerable to global demands in two areas: foreign policy and domestic policy".[123]

The Political Strategy of Defence

What was the defence policy of the apartheid regime? The defence policy of South Africa, like any other defence policy, was designed in conformity with the context, threats, challenges, and abilities of the state. Therefore, to understand the defence policy, we need to do an analytic regression to contextualize the data. It is evident that the fundamental efforts in the field of defence policy began after the Second World War, as they considered the time lapse from 1946 to 1956 as *demobilisation and reorganisation*.[124] They called the period from 1957 to 1959 *consolidation*. At this time, they approved Defence Act No. 44 of 1957. This law was the base that allowed restructuring the Union Defence Force (UDF), giving way to the South Africa Defence Forces (SADF).[125] This military reform happened four years before the proclamation of the Republic of South Africa (1961), and it introduced significant changes. But the proclamation of the Republic, inspired in the ideas of nationalist Afrikaners, was the object of condemnation. Thereafter, the country faced the first weapons embargo. Furthermore, change

---

[122] Anton du Plessis, 1997, 19.
[123] Robert Scire and Daniel Silke, 1997, 4.
[124] *Militaria*, 1987, 16.
[125] Idem, 18.

was then visible in "conventional war to forms of non-conventional and insurgency war".[126] Due to these realities, the South African State decided to manoeuvre. The period from 1960 to 1970 is thus called *modernisation and expansion*.[127] The armed forces began being adjusted from top to bottom, considering internal and external challenges.[128]

In the scope of the changes in the SADF, the way of providing national military service changed. In 1970 they enlisted many citizens.[129] Hence the land forces, navy, and air force grew in staff and also combat means. The defence budget was also changed. For this period the estimated military expenditure was 272 million rands, according to the Defence Department of South Africa[130].

The period from 1971 to 1975 was called *challenge and response*, as South Africa, from early 1970, faced isolation, external threats, and anti-apartheid campaigns. Conventional and non-conventional war had increased, and the SADF had to act in conformity with the challenges.[131] In the period reviewed, the Defence Department of South Africa published the *White Paper of 1973*, outlining the missions of the SADF.[132] This white paper includes the guiding lines of the defence policy:

The RSA's General Defence Policy with a View to the Future[133]

> 10. As clearly indicated above, the task of the South African Defence Force does not entail a threat to any other country. Therefore, our posture is defensive and not offensive. Defence, however, cannot be merely passive; our policy thus demands a measure of retaliatory capability.

---

[126] Idem, 19.
[127] Idem, 19-20.
[128] In this period, the Defence Forces of South Africa intervened in Angola in the context of counter-insurgency of the Armed Forces of Portugal.
[129] See *Oorsic oor Verdediging en Krygstuigproduksie Tydprerk 1960 tot 1970*, 6.
[130] Idem, 8.
[131] *Militaria*, op. cit., 20.
[132] *White Paper*, 1973, 5.
[133] Emphasis added.

11. The RSA cannot engage in an arms race with the rest of the world. Therefore, our defence is concentrated not so much on quantity as on quality balance. One of our most important objectives is constant preparedness in both the material and spiritual sense. Despite modern weapons the individual soldier remains the most important factor in the defence of our country and its people.

12. The Defence Force is continuing with its efforts to achieve the greatest possible degree of standardization, rationalization, and independence in the supply and maintenance of armaments.

13. The Ten Year Programme for the Future. Although, over the years, a high degree of preparedness has been reached, certain essential facilities and items of major equipment needed to attain the optimum of our objectives, are still lacking. To this end a ten-year programme was submitted to the Government in 1970 by the Chiefs of the Defence Force and was approved by the Government. The further development of the Defence Force is proceeding, and will for the next few years proceed, mainly in accordance with this programme, but regular revision and modification will obviously be necessary to keep in step with circumstances and the threats against the RSA.[134]

Upon analysing the defence policy, they acknowledged there had been progress since 1969 and concluded that there was a need to proceed with modernisation. To do this, they paid special attention to the reorganisation of the command, the control structures, and the articulation between the state bodies that dealt with defence matters.

---

[134] *White Paper on Defence and Armament Production*, 1973, 6.

They also improved decision-making support bodies at the highest level. Between 1969 and 1973, the budget for defence was 4.8 per cent of the total gross domestic product. They planned to spend 534 million rands to purchase means of combat and other equipment.[135] Meanwhile, in 1975, the SADF reassessed the international and regional situation. They concluded there was a need to adapt the Defence Forces to the new political headwinds. Hence the *White Paper* of 1975 highlighted, namely, the following points:

> 15. Developments in Neighbouring States. It is universally hoped that the situation in Angola and Mozambique will develop to a state of stability and good neighbourliness and that Rhodesia's problems will be solved. The signs are encouraging but there are apparently also undesirable influences and tendencies. The situation in the political and economic fields therefore remains fluid and it is essential that our defence strategy provides for all contingencies....
>
> 17. Revolutionary forces regard the Portuguese developments as an important victory. In conformity with the Marxist dialectics concerning balance of power, this therefore represents to them a significant shift of the centre of gravity in their favour. This will undoubtedly encourage the radical elements in revolutionary organisations inside and outside the R.S.A. and incite them to greater efforts. They regard Angola and Mozambique as new allies and potential new operational bases for action against Rhodesia and the R.S.A.[136]

Facing predictable changes in the geopolitical atmosphere of Southern Africa, the political leadership of that country, as per

---

[135] *White Paper on Defence and Armament Production*, 1973, 7.
[136] Idem.

the present white paper, stressed that its "strategic policy remained unchangeable" and gave indications to the SADF. They thus adjusted the system of national military service and introduced the voluntary military service subsystem as an extension of the military service system. A review of the defence expenditure revealed it was 989 million rands for 1975 and 1976, equivalent to 4.1 per cent of the country's general expenditure. But in the previous period, 1974–75, expenditure had reached 707 million rands.[137] With those expenses, South Africa wished to keep its defence forces at the highest level, remove obsolete means of combat, and acquire new equipment.

The time span from 1976 to 1987 was deemed the *contemporary South African Defence Force*.[138] This was a period of structural transformations within the military organisation, to improve the levels of readiness and combat efficiency.[139] In the 1977 white paper, P. W. Botha, as the minister of defence, stressed that "developments in Southern Africa and the international sphere had deeply influenced the factors that [affected] the total strategy of South Africa, its policies, the level of military forces and required defence expenditure".[140] Moreover, they drafted the total national strategy on the basis of these considerations.

The SADF took the principle that the "scales of power in Southern Africa [was] fluid. However, the structure of the force [should] be flexible enough to adapt within certain limits and without major changes to the new developments in the field of political security."[141] Due to this attitude, military expenditure from 1975 to 1976 reached a value of 1 billion and 43 million rands, which represented 4.1 per cent of gross domestic product. In the following year, 1976–77, values were set at 1 billion and 407 million rands. In 1977–78, the figure increased to 1 billion 700 million rands, equivalent to 19 per cent of the state expenditure.[142] These values show the amounts employed in defence and associated areas.

---

[137] *White Paper on Defence and Armament Production*, 1973, 9.
[138] *Militaria*, 21.
[139] Idem, 22.
[140] *White Paper on Defence 1977*, 3
[141] Idem, 10.
[142] Idem, 12.

In 1979, they reassessed the situation of national security and the behaviour of the great powers. They re-examined the threats to the country as well as the conflict over the independence of Southwest Africa and preparation of the South Africa Defence Forces to counter dangers and guarantee a safe and peaceful life. They also scrutinised the planning of national defence and privileged coordination between departments in the scope of the total national strategy. As for the defence forces, they defined that the planning process should be executed bearing in mind forces appointed, force development, and application force. This type of force was responsible for the execution of strategies, missions, and tasks of the SADF. This force had a flexible structure and material and financial means that were always available.[143]

To continue strengthening the defence system, in 1980 national military service was extended to twenty-four months. The voluntary service went from twelve to eighteen or twenty-four months. This type of military service now included "white young women", "coloured and Indian population groups", and blacks. The inclusion of all races in the defence forces was an initiative of Magnus Malan, as chief of the defence forces. It was he that defined the principle of "human dignity" within the military rank and file, mainly in areas of responsibility within the defence forces.[144] The civilian component also had staff from every population group.[145] Nevertheless, defence expenditure reached 1 billion 583 million (1977–78), 1 billion 759 million (1978–79) and 1 billion 972 million (1979–80).[146] With increasing military operations, expenditure significantly escalated and continued growing vertiginously. Between 1980 and 1981, the reference value was 2 billion rands. In 1988–89, most expenses were set as 8 billion rands.[147]

During the period in question, they also took another measure to reinforce the national security system. They approved a new civilian

---

[143] See *White Paper on Defence and Armaments Supply 1979*, 1–2.
[144] Magnus Malan, 2006, 176. He wrote in his memoir: "Instruction made it clear that all Defence Force members, irrespective of gender or colour, where to be treated with dignity" (sic).
[145] Idem, 3–4.
[146] Idem, 12.
[147] Ian van der Waag, 2015, 270.

defence law: Law 67 of 1977. This law granted powers to provincial municipalities to take care of defence in their areas of jurisdiction and to take full responsibility for security. Hence civilian defence was structured and equipped with means.[148]

In the following years, the conceptual lines of the defence policy remained valid, but Magnus Malan propelled political power to reach an understanding concerning the employment of the defence forces in neighbouring countries. Therefore, political power granted freedom to the chief of defence to carry out military actions within 150 km inside Angolan territory. He also obtained a green light from the South African government for the air force to carry out operations inside Angola within 100 km.[149] He pursued similar efforts as minister of defence of the Republic of South Africa.[150]

They conceived the defence policy under scrutiny in accordance with the political conception of the apartheid regime and its interests. They projected several strategies in conformity with the stages that the defence forces went through. Besides, the defence policy defined the types and level of force and allocated funds for the military budgets in accordance with the aims selected (command and control, land forces,

---

[148] Idem, 15.
[149] Magnus Malan, 2006, 173. But in 1985, during a visit by a United Nations enquiry commission to Angola, Magnus Malan made a public statement. See "Statement by the Minister of Defence, General Magnus Malan, 1985, Declassified, 2008-02-05".
[150] Idem. He highlights: "Later, in my capacity as Minister of Defence, I compiled a written policy document concerning crosser-border operations for consideration by the Government. This document was approved by a resolution of the Cabinet under the chairmanship of the Prime Minister, P. W. Botha. Various policy prescriptions applicable to possible cross-border operations from South Africa and South West Africa, and aimed at various neighbouring countries, were formulated and updated regularly. The following was taken into account in formulating each policy prescription for action against each neighbouring state: its political and military attitude; probable actions; the attitude of the neighbouring country concerned towards South Africa; aid to, protection and support to enemy elements; and covert or overt approval of the use of its territory by enemy elements." (173–74).

air defence, maritime defence, general training, logistical support, staff support, general support, and civilian defence).[151]

The military policy of South Africa was conceived in conformity with the total national strategy, but listed the military aims as follows:

a. The development of the national defence structure necessary to prevent and/or counter any threat to the RSA.
b. The defence and security of the RSA and its body politic against any form of external aggression or internal revolution, irrespective of its source of origin, with all the forces at our command.
c. The involvement of the entire nation in the maintenance of law and order and in the defence of the RSA.
d. Assistance and support to independent Black homelands, if requested, in developing their own defence forces, for the security of their territories, the maintenance of law and order and the assurance of their independence.[152]

Regarding military policy, they said: "the policy of the South Africa Defence Forces, within the targets, aims and policies of the State, is the following":

a. The RSA must, as far as practicable, be self-sufficient in the provision of arms and ensure their continued production.
b. Provision must be made for effective counter-insurgency warfare of short or long duration.
c. The major striking power of the Defence Force is based on a part-time with a strong Permanent Force nucleus to provide specialist leadership.
d. The Defence Force must develop an adequate conventional capability, defencelessness of the RSA and as a warning to potential aggressors.

---

[151] P. S. Botes, 1979, 15–20.
[152] *White Paper on Defence 1977*, 9.

Miguel Júnior

- e. The Defence Force must be ready to give immediate support to the SA Police in the maintenance of internal law and order.
- f. The Defence Force must be ready at a moment's notice to support the civil infra-structure in the preservation of lives, health or property and the maintenance of essential services.
- g. The Defence Force must maintain and develop an efficient intelligence network in order to contribute to the efforts of the national intelligence services in determining the scope and nature of the military or any other threat.
- h. The Defence Force must be capable of operating in any part of the RSA and, under the Defence Act, in neighbouring states.
- i. The Defence Force must be maintained and enlarged to form a highly mobile force for immediate action at any moment.
- j. All operations be guided and carried out in a decisive way.[153]

Here are listed the fundamental points of the military policy of the Republic of South Africa, which guided the life and activities of its defence forces.[154] A proactive attitude was visible in this military policy. Malan, who led the South Africa Defence Forces (SADF) and was later on minister of Defence, explains that it was he that suggested that minister of defence P. W. Botha change the attitude of the defence forces as soon as he took office as head of the defence forces in 1976, that is, one year before the publication of the 1977 white paper.

Moreover, Magnus Malan, in his autobiography *My Life with the SA Defence Force*, stressed: "the Government heeded my request to alter the profile from defensive to proactive, as it was of national interest to approve proactive action to preserve national security. This change to a proactive attitude was one of the reasons why no war ruin is found in

---

[153] *White Paper on Defence 1977*, 9.
[154] Under that military policy, South African society was militarised in different levels. Militarisation covered all spheres of national life. This situation arose from the fact that military power defended the interests of a minority and extensively used its coercive power. The defence forces were used in large scale internally. From 1984 to 1986, the military forces were used extensively. See *War and Society: The Militarisation of South Africa*, Jacklyn Cock and Laurie Nathan, 1989.

South Africa."[155] He means that this was the best choice. But the idea that "no ruin of war is found in South Africa" is absurd and incorrect. In fact, in South Africa there are no war ruins from the point of view of infrastructures. But within its territory human ruins abounded. Inside South Africa, millions of human beings lived in subhuman conditions and without dignity. This was the big social and political fracture of South Africa, which corroded the state and shook the foundations of the apartheid system. Moreover, Sampie Terreblanche, South African academician emeritus in the field of economy, writes in his work *A History of Inequality in South Africa 1652–2002*:

> It deals with the highly unequal distribution on income, opportunities, and property that has marked South Africa for so long; however, it deals mainly with the unequal distribution of political, economic, and ideological power that has become so deeply embedded in our society and has shaped and reshaped it in such unfortunate ways from 1652 to 2002.
>
> Unequal power structures played a central role during South Africa's long colonial period (from 1652 to 1910). This trend continued during the period of segregation and apartheid (from 1910 to 1994), when power was entirely monopolised by whites—with devastating consequences for blacks. Unfortunately, unequal power relations and unequal socio-economic outcomes have remained defining characteristic of the post-Apartheid period. Despite our transition to an inclusive democracy, old forms of inequality have been perpetuated, and some entrenched more deeply than ever before.[156]

---

[155] Magnus Malan, 2006, 170–172.
[156] Sampie Terreblanche, 2002, xv.

This excerpt explains the historic roots of inequality within South African society and highlights the fact that during the apartheid regime, inequality was felt with "devastating consequences for blacks", with deep impact on the present.

Having explained the military policy of the Republic of South Africa, let us approach another relevant point of the total national strategy of this country: the strategic doctrines.

The Strategic Doctrines

Bearing in mind the targets, aims and policies of the Republic of South Africa, and having identified the threats that it faces, the grounds that are the basis for the strategic doctrines of the South Africa Defence Forces may be summarised:

> *Defence Posture.* Our posture is based on the Government's firm policy of non-aggression towards any other country or group; that we have no ambitions in terms of territorial expansion and that we wish to live in peace and co-operation with neighbouring states. Obviously, this does not imply that we will tolerate any aggression against us; our posture is, therefore, defensive but prepared. In the event of an attack, the SA Defence Force possesses, however, both the means and the will to defend its territorial integrity by fighting a conventional offensive battle against any aggressor.
>
> *Deterrence.* As a counter to the possibility of any attack against the RSA by conventional forces it is considered that a credible deterrent is the best means of discouraging such intentions on the part of any potential aggressor. For this purpose the RSA maintains a balanced Army, Air Force and Navy, equipped with the most modern weapons available to us, and extensive

use is made of modern military technology. As far as manpower is concerned, the emphasis is placed at all levels, especially in respect of training, leadership and motivation.

Counter-Insurgency. Thwarting insurgency and maintaining the authority of the elected government requires an indirect strategy, in which military force is but a single facet, for terrorism is only one of the means used by the insurgents to achieve their aims. Nonetheless, the military role is of the utmost importance and much attention is devoted by the SA Defence Force to the study and implementation of counter-insurgency.

Assistance to Civil Authorities. The SA Defence Force is ready at all times to support the civil authorities in the maintenance of law and order, and to provide such help as may be sought with regard to the preservation of lives, health and property, and maintenance of essential services throughout the RSA.[157]

We will now examine the contents of the four points that were the strategic doctrines of the South Africa Defence Forces. Beginning with defence, it mirrored the guidelines of the defence policy. Meanwhile, a defensive attitude means an attitude of strength. This may be weak and low profile or ambitious, that is, aggressive.[158] For that matter, the SADF chose an aggressive attitude, as per the total national strategy and statements by Magnus Malan. The use of force was a constant, in conformity with the purposes of the defence forces and in accordance with its proactive attitude.

They evidently declared that dissuasion would be carried out using their conventional forces as a whole (meaning the army, air force, and navy). These would be used to fight the armed branches of the

---

[157] *White Paper on Defence 1977*, 10.
[158] Michael H. H. Louw, 1978.

liberation movements (ANC, SWAPO, and PAC) and to stop armed action against their territory. Moreover, General C. L. Viljoen, chief of the SADF, stressed in his reflection Conventional Threat to the RSA and SWA that there was "a fundamental wish in certain black African States to attack the R.S.A. with conventional weapons".[159]

To demonstrate that wish, he used empirical data of six years (1977–83) to prove that neighbouring countries had increased their conventional means: troops in "300%" ("270 400 00" men), "10% of which were Cuban, soviet and Eastern German forces"; likewise, there was a "300% [increase] of tanks" and "200% of aircraft".[160] This reflection certainly lacked discernment, however, because he emphasised that "African countries (individually or collectively)" had no "real offensive military [capacity] to threaten the Republic of South Africa".[161]

Still regarding the conventional dissuasion of South Africa, D. J. Mortimer, a defence forces brigadier general, made critical remarks in the paper "Conventional Deterrence with Specific Reference to the RSA", saying that "dissuasion is, in fact, possible only if nations have nuclear weapons".[162] This means, according to his point of view, that South African conventional dissuasion should evolve to a nuclear deterrent or otherwise be based solely on nuclear deterrent. In fact, according to strategic theories, dissuasion evolved and gained a new dimension because of the emergence of nuclear weapons.

The question arises: Did South Africa already possess nuclear weapons? The answer is yes, and there is data on the matter that explains how the country achieved that feat. This gain went through different stages, as Al. J. Venter explains in his book *How South Africa Built Six Atom Bombs*.[163] The author points out in chapter 10 ("The Search for

---

[159] C. L. Viljoen, 1983, 4.
[160] Idem, 6–7.
[161] Idem, 7.
[162] D. J. Mortimer, 2–6.
[163] Al. J. Venter, 2008. Another work that deals with the production of nuclear weapons by South Africa is *Die Bom* by Nic von Wielligh and Lydia von Wielligh-Steyn (2014).

a Tactical Nuclear Weapon): "Operation Savannah—long months of South African incursion in 1975 and 1976 in Angola, which collapsed into total chaos even before the Portuguese withdrawal—ended in ignominy when the small South African intervention force withdrew. One result of that brief campaign was acceleration in the acquisition of nuclear weapons."[164] From this moment the political and military authorities accelerated their programmes in search of nuclear capacity, which allowed evolving to the nuclear deterrent.

Facing this reality, cogitations gained form inside and outside the country. Thus M. Hough made an incursion on the matter in the paper "The Political Implications of the Possession of Nuclear Weapons for South Africa", reflecting on the advantages, disadvantages, and political implications of owning nuclear weapons. In his view, conventional dissuasion was "more adequate to the regional and continental context".[165] But the nuclear deterrent was of value with an opponent whose escalation went to the "level of nuclear strategy". According to him, the development of nuclear weapons could increase criticism against South Africa, as was already the case, due to the aggressions that it carried out in the regional context.[166]

In practice, South Africa had a nuclear doctrine. But the details of the nuclear doctrine were made public only after the situation evolved in the late eighties, with the end of armed conflict in Southern Africa. In 1990, President F. W. de Klerk addressed a letter to President George H. W. Bush of the United States of America to guarantee that South Africa had committed to nuclear disarmament and that he would declare "South Africa a zone free of nuclear weapons".[167] With the resolution of the conflict in Southern Africa, and with the end of the apartheid regime in 1993, as leader of the National Party, F. W. de Klerk finally produced the declaration in the South African Parliament, in the following terms:

---

[164] Idem, 143.
[165] M. Hough, 1980, 8.
[166] Idem.
[167] See "Letter from South African President de Klerk to President Bush", Wilson Centre, Digital Archive International History Declassified, August 31, 1990.

At one stage, South Africa did, indeed, develop a limited nuclear deterrent capability.

The decision to develop this limited capability was taken as early as 1974, against the background of a Soviet expansionist threat in Southern Africa, as well as prevailing uncertainty concerning the designs of the Warsaw Pact members.

The build-up of the Cuban forces in Angola from 1975 onward reinforced the perception that a deterrent was necessary—as did South Africa's relative international isolation and the fact that it could not rely on outside assistance, should it be attacked.

Details relating to the limited deterrent capability, and the strategy in this regard, which were at that time developed, are as follows:

The objective was the provision of seven nuclear fission devices which was considered the minimum for testing purposes and for the maintenance thereafter of credible deterrent capability;

When the decision was taken to terminate the programme, only six devices had been completed;

No advanced nuclear explosives, such as thermonuclear explosives, were manufactured;

The programme was under the direct control of the Head of Government, who decided that it should be managed and implemented by Armscor;

Knowledge of the existence of the programme was limited to a number of Ministers on a "need-to-know" basis;

The strategy was that, if the situation in Southern Africa were to deteriorate seriously, a confidential indication of the deterrent capability would be given to one or more of the major Powers, for example the United States, in attempt to persuade to intervene;

There was never an intention of using devices and from the start emphasis was put on dissuasion;

During 1989, the global political situation changed dramatically:

A cease-fire in Angola was agreed;

On 22 December 1988, a tripartite agreement was signed at the United Nations with Cuba and Angola which provides for the independence of Namibia and the withdrawal of 50,000 troops from Angola;

The cold war had come to an end and developments leading to the destruction of the Berlin Wall and the breakup of the Soviet bloc had become the order of the day;

The prospects of moving away from a confrontational relationship with the international community in general and with our neighbours in Africa, in particular, to one cooperation and development were good;

In these circumstances a nuclear deterrent had become, not only superfluous, but in fact an obstacle to the development of South Africa's international relations.[168]

In 1993, F. W. de Klerk made these revelations and showed the path that South Africa should follow in regional and international contexts. After de Klerk's revelations and after a statement about nuclear weapons that made Armscor (the corporation responsible for South Africa's nuclear development), on 29 March 1993, John Carlin published. "Pretoria was close to launching a nuclear bomb in Luanda: with troops under pressure in Angola; South Africa feared the worst."[169] The clashes peaked in 1987. South African despair was evident, as John Carlin describes in his opinion paper.

Nevertheless, the issue of employing nuclear weapons in an atmosphere of limited war or the possibility of a preventive nuclear strike requires other considerations. The situation resulted in the first time in history that the use of nuclear weapons was considered within a limited war. It was the first time that, in an atmosphere of limited war, the use of nuclear weapons with "limited dissuasion capacity" was expected and the first time in the African continent that "emphasis" was put in nuclear dissuasion.

The idea of "limited dissuasion capacity" is, ultimately, the so-called "*stratégie du déterrent minimum*" in conformity with the vision of the strategy general André Beaufre's classic. The implied meaning is that

---

[168] F. W. de Klerk, 1993, "Speech in Joint Session of Parliament on Accession to the Non-Proliferation Treaty", 3–4. See "Speech by South African President F. W. de Klerk to a Joint Session of Parliament on Accession to the Non-Proliferation Treaty, Wilson Centre Digital International History Declassified, March 24, 1993". Jade Davenport clarifies that "the factor that most impelled the government to construct a nuclear weapons arsenal was its belief that, because of the international isolation that stemmed from its consistent refusal to reform its policy of apartheid, in an event of an attack or an invasion, it would not be to rely on foreign military assistance". See *Digging Deep: A History of Mining in South Africa*, 2013, 456.

[169] See John Carlin, in www.independent.co.uk/news/, 1–10. See the text by the author titled: "Pretoria came close to dropping nuclear bomb on Luanda: With troops under pressure in Angola, South Africa feared the worst", writes John Carlin in Johannesburg, Monday, 29 March 1993.

if an opponent follows through with political intentions, a "terrible punishment" will follow.[170]

The theory of nuclear deterrence clearly describes how it is implemented. But the strategies of nuclear deterrence are conceived against opponents that have the same capacities. Angola did not have nuclear weapons, and neither did its ally Cuba. Nor was the Soviet Union, as a superpower and ally of Angola, interested in supporting escalation to high levels with the possibility of employing nuclear means. But the situation regarding a preventive nuclear strike by South Africa proves that actors involved in a limited war may face a strike of that nature if escalation reaches higher operational levels. This may happen due to lack of perception of the enemy's intentions and due to uncertainty and fear. General António Barrento (2010), following the spirit of the reflection of general André Beaufre (1963), said "that *fear* is the base of dissuasion, *uncertainty* is the guarantee of nuclear deterrent".[171]

In accordance with events in Southern Africa during the South Africa–Angola war, a limited nuclear strike may be effective if rationality is missing from the actors involved therein. Hence the African continent, especially Southern Africa, would have experienced nuclear strike resulting from the "limited dissuasion capacity" of the Republic of South Africa, as per the statements expressed by the political leader of the National Party, F. W. de Klerk.

A 30 August 1988 report-opinion by the Department of Foreign Affairs of South Africa about Armscor and the country's nuclear capacity discussed the situation of war in Southern Africa and the probability that escalation would result. The report reviewed the situation from the standpoint of the strategy of uncertainty.[172]

The South Africa Defence Forces declared that the study and implementation of counter-insurgency was among their priorities to

---

[170] André Beaufre, 1963, 110.
[171] António Barrento, 2010, 233.
[172] See report, South African Department of Foreign Affairs, "A Balanced Approach to the NPT: ARMSCOR/AEC Concerns Viewed from a DFA Standpoint", Wilson Centre, Digital Archive, International History Declassified, 01 September 1988.

counter revolutionary forces. The truth is that they already had an elaborate theory for that purpose. Records show it, and the realities experienced reinforce the present affirmation. Diving into the records, C. A. Fraser, a South African general, conceived the counter-insurgency manual "Lessons Learnt from Past Revolutionary Wars" in the early 1960s, when John Vorster was prime minister of the country. That work, as Christi van der Westhuizen says, "gained popularity in South African security circles during the 60s" and was the basis for formulating the "counter-revolutionary strategy of the Government of the National Party".[173] Based on the principles of that work, they carried out from beginning to end the whole counter-insurgency activity of Southwest Africa and provided support to the military forces of Rhodesia and Portugal in Angola and Mozambique. These were the realities.

---

[173] Christi van der Westhuizen, 2007, 104. But the work of general C. A. Fraser, as we could see in an original copy, was called "Lessons Learnt from Past Revolutionary Wars"; thereafter, submitted to review, it was called *Revolutionary Warfare: Basic Principles of Counter-Insurgency.*

CHAPTER 3

The Evolution of War and the Changes

This chapter is about the evolution of war and the changes that took place inside South Africa. To begin, it outlines the modality of strategic action of this state given the interests at stake and the change that took place due to internal, regional and international developments. It closes with the end of the apartheid regime.

The Modality of Strategic Action

This investigation in the field of the total national strategy of South Africa allowed identifying the method of strategic planning adopted and the way that the strategy itself was structured. And it allowed devising the modality of strategic action. The total national strategy of South Africa fits into the modality of direct strategy, although from a doctrinaire point of view, the defensive attitude prevailed. Direct strategy is palpable since all efforts were concentrated towards making war.

War was a real fact against certain countries of Southern Africa, mainly Angola (1975–89). Threats of war were also constant against all that opposed their wishes in Southern Africa. The attitude of war was closely associated with their political-strategic goal: defending the apartheid system. Thus, the military strategy worked to reach the strategic-military aim. On this basis, military campaigns were aimed at disassembling the opposing military forces in the region in order to make survival of apartheid easier as a political-strategic aim. The military strategy obfuscated all other strategies (Benjamin Disraeli, 2017, 140).[174] Other strategies worked as appendixes of the military strategy. The proof is visible in the political-diplomatic strategy (James Barber and John Bart, 1990).[175] In this view, a military strategy was the dominant strategy to defend their interests, especially to safeguard their political strategic aim: apartheid. In other words, war was the instrument used to maintain the *status quo*. They waged war against the revolutionary forces (ANC, SWAPO and PAC) and against states that opposed their aims, particularly Angola.

But direct strategy has two essential manoeuvres to be successful and achieve its political-strategic aim. One is internal and the other is an external, but both are articulated in conformity with the situations.

We shall nevertheless show other opinions. G. C. Olivier (1983, 379), in his reflection "Strategy and Tactics for Change in South Africa", highlights that "South Africa is itself presently in a situation of quick and potential social disorder and economic and political change".[176] In turn, David Welsh (2009, 172–207) describes the "Fissures and Fractures in Afrikaner Nationalism" in his book *The Rise and Fall of Apartheid*. At the time, Afrikaners were divided, disunited, and not following all that their political and religious leaders said. Among Afrikaner intellectuals and scholars, challenges to the practices of the National Party were evident. Such changes were because "Afrikaners were highly urbanised, better educated than previous generations". Some circles of Afrikaner youth also disagreed with certain practices. Besides, the economic and social problems grew due to the situation of insecurity felt all throughout the country.

On the other hand, South African society was militarised at every level and domain. Gavin Evans (1989, 283–97) states that high school

---

[174] This author explains that the "Defence Force's growing involvement in policy making has been the product of the security situation in Southern Africa. See Deon Geldenhuys, *The Diplomacy of Isolation South African Foreign Policy Making*, 2017.
[175] See *South Africa's Foreign Policy: The Search for Status and Security*, 1945–88.
[176] See *Change in South Africa*, D. J. van Vuurem et al., 1983.

and university students underwent military preparation.[177] At the time, South African society already faced the *People's War* (Anthea Jeffry, 2009)[178]. This represented a new stage in the struggle of the African people of South Africa for their emancipation under the leadership of ANC.

Meanwhile, Miguel Júnior (2012) used data produced by Anthea Jeffry and crossed it with other data from the University of Pretoria's Institute for Strategic Studies to draft the opinion paper titled: "Apartheid and the People's War."[179] Because of that new form of war taking place in South Africa, fear and insecurity reigned. A report titled "Unrest Situation in South Africa: September 1984–May 1987" makes the facts evident:

> Since September 1984, South Africa has experienced a serious wave of violence and unrest. In order to counter the escalating violence, a National State of Emergency (NSE) was declared by the State President on June 12, 1986. The State President stated that three main aims were to be served by the NSE, namely a return to stability by restoring law and order; a return to normality; and the continuation of the reform process.[180]

It's easy to see herein the critical situation from the internal point of view and the intention of state president P. W. Botha to carry out

---

[177] In his text *Classrooms of War: The Militarisation of White South African Schooling*, he writes: "Once a week over 300,000 white South African youth leave their school uniforms at home and come to class in military browns. For an hour or more a week, they learn the basics of army drill, how to shoot and more advanced forms of 'military preparedness.… These activities include Youth Preparedness programmes, the veldschools in the Transvaal, civil defence exercises, school guidance programmes and more recently the emergency anti-terrorist plan' initiated by the Joint Management Centres", 1989, 283.

[178] *People's War: New Light on the Struggle for South Africa*, 2009.

[179] See "Apartheid and the People's War" (*Jornal de Angola*, 20 March 2012, 12, History Archive).

[180] ISSUP, Strategic Review, August 1987, 21.

political reform in order to make compatible the interests of the majority that had been subjugated by the apartheid regime. The idea of reforming society was patent in different political, economic, social, cultural, religious, and intellectual quarters, but the question was how things would progress. Would it be by "evolution or revolutionary change" (F. L. Acron and R. D. Henwood, 1990, 14–35)?[181] These data show that the internal manoeuvre was difficult because South African society was fractured. Articulating the total national strategy of South Africa was difficult due to several obstacles, namely: the critical domestic political situation, social divisions, clashes, and divided internal public opinion. In short, the political line chosen did not favour the internal manoeuvre.

From the point of view of the external manoeuvre, the situation was worse. The state was isolated and excluded from the international system. The war that the state waged against Angola and the military developments in the war theatre much worsened its condition. The external manoeuvre was taking place without any space to move. The direct strategy taken to the highest level made it harder.

The Strategic Change and the End of Apartheid

The South African State was trapped with its total national strategy. Inside the National Party, divisions were more than evident, and they led to the internal reform of the party. P. W. Botha left politics and the leadership of the state and the party because it was hard for him to implement reform. John Cameron-Dow (2016, 63) stresses that "Botha's reform policies did not offer a potential long-term solution". The situation was deadlocked, and there was a need to progress. The forces of change, under the leadership of F. W. de Klerk, took notice of the situation. The alternative was the solution negotiated for the regional conflict and the internal problems. For the actors involved in the regional armed conflict, the understanding implied agreeing on

---

[181] ISSUP, Strategic Review, November 1990.

"Principles for a peaceful settlement in south-western Africa" (1988).[182] After that, the parties signed other agreements (New York Agreement, 1988). Meanwhile, the liberation of Nelson Mandela helped consolidate the process of political transition until the first democratic elections were held in South Africa. Recalling the clashes in Angola in 1987, Nelson Mandela (1991) said:

> The crushing defeat of the racist army at Cuito Cuanavale was a victory for the whole of Africa!
>
> The overwhelming defeat of the racist army at Cuito Cuanavale provided the possibility for Angola to enjoy peace and consolidate its own sovereignty!
>
> The defeat of racist army allowed the struggling people of Namibia to finally win … their independence!
>
> The decisive defeat of the Apartheid aggressors broke the myth of the invincibility of the white oppressors!
>
> The defeat of the Apartheid army was an inspiration to the struggling people inside South Africa.
>
> Without the defeat of Cuito Cuanavale our organisation would not been unbanned! …
>
> Cuito Cuanavale was a milestone in the history of the struggle for Southern African liberation! Cuito Cuanavale has been a turning point in the struggle to free the continent and our country from the scourge of apartheid![183]

---

[182] See the agreement between Angola, Cuba, and South Africa "Principles for a peaceful settlement in South-western Africa", Wilson Centre, Digital Archive, International History Declassified, July 20, 1988.
[183] *Nelson Mandela and Fidel Castro—How Far We Slaves Have Come*, 1991, 25.

The total national strategy of South Africa failed. The strategic inflection engendered by F. W. de Klerk and the strategic positioning of Nelson Mandela resurrected the dreams of thousands of South Africans of all persuasions. They inaugurated a new era in the history of South Africa. But South Africans acknowledge the inputs of Angola, Cuba, and other countries to the cause of a new South Africa (Oliver Tambo, 2014, 22).[184]

---

[184] See Oliver Tambo, address to the First Congress of the MPLA, Luanda, December 1977.

Conclusions

In this research work about the total national strategy of South Africa, we have reviewed the strategic positioning of this country from 1948 to 1994. The then-existing strategy was meant to safeguard the apartheid regime and its interests, but it faced the struggle of South African fighters that longed for political change and a society free from racial segregation. The fight against apartheid was supported by forces from the whole world, and many voices were raised to condemn that hideous system of racial segregation. The total national strategy failed before the determination of all progressive forces and lovers of freedom, justice, and equality, and in favour of human rights. Indeed, victory provided South Africans with a fairer society, one that is balanced and democratic. South Africa is in peace, as is the region of Southern Africa as a whole.

From the point of view of strategic thought and strategic studies, the period under review provides numerous lessons. From the point of view of war and its studies, we have also recorded useful teachings. One of them is that war is won strategically. That condition is necessary to achieve the political-strategic aim pursued in any given war. The apartheid regime lost the war.

Bibliography

Authors

Various Authors. 1997. *Change and South African External Relations.* Southern Africa: International Thomson Publishing Pty Ltd.

Various Authors. 1989. South Africa and Its Neighbours Regional Security and Self-Interest. The World Peace Foundation.

Barber, James and John Bart. 2011. *South Africa's Foreign Policy: The Search for Status and Security 1948–1988*, Cambridge: Cambridge University Press.

Barrento, António. 2010. *Da Estratégia,* Tribuna da História. Lisbon.

Barrroso, Luís. 2012. "Salazar, Caetano e o Reduto Branco, A Manobra Político-Diplomática de Portugal na África Austral (1951–1974)". Porto: Fronteira do Caos Editores.

Basson, J. L. 1980. *J G Strijdom Sy Politieke Loopbaan van 1929 tot 1948*, Pretoria-Wes: Gedruk deur Sigma Press.

Beaufre, André. 1963. *Introduction à La Stratégie.* Paris: Hachette Littératures.

Berridge, G. R. 1992. South Africa, the Colonial Powers, and "African Defence": The Rise and Fall of the White Entente, 1948-60. London: The Macmillan Press Ltd.

Callaghy, Thomas M. 1983. South Africa in Southern Africa: The Intensifying Vortex of Violence. New York: Praeger Publishers.

Carlsnaes, Walter, and Marie Muller. 1997. *Change and South Africa External Relations*, South Africa: International Thompson Publishing Pty Ltd.

Cock, Jacklyn, and Laurie Nathan. 1989. *War and Society: The Militarisation of South Africa*. New York: David Philip Pty Ltd.

Couper, Scott. 2012. *TITLE?* Scottsville: University of KwaZulu-Natal Press.

Davenport, Jade. 2013. *Digging Deep: A History of Mining in South Africa*, Jeppestown: Jonathan Ball Publishers Ltd.

Davenport, Rodney and Christopher Sauders. 2002. *South Africa: A Modern History*. New York: St. Martin's Press, Inc.

D'Oliveira, John. 1977. *Vorster—The Man*. Johannesburg: Ernest Stanton Pty Ltd.

Dye, Thomas R. 2002. *Understanding Public Policy*. New Jersey: Prentice Hall.

Doyle, Arthur Conan. 1999. *The Great Boer War*. Alberton: Galago Books.

Fraser, C. A. n.d. Revolutionary Warfare: Basic Principles of Counter-Insurgency.

Jeffery, Anthea. 2009. *People's War: New Light on the Struggle for South Africa*. Jeppestown: Jonathan Ball Publishers Pty Ltd.

Garcia, Francisco Proença. 2010. *A Guerra de Moçambique 1964-1974*. Lisbon: Author and QuidNovi.

Garnett, J. C. "National Security and Threat Perception". *ISSUP Strategic Review* (November 1989): 1—38.

Geldenhuys, D. J. "The International Isolation of South Africa". *ISSUP Strategic Review* (May 1989): 39–59.

Geldenhuys, Deon. 2017. *The Diplomacy of Isolation: South African Foreign Policy Making*. Johannesburg: South African Institute of International Affairs.

Giliomee, Hermann. 2012. *The Afrikaners Biography of a People*. Cape Town: Tafelberg.

Giliomee, Hermann. 2012. The Last Afrikaner Leaders: A Supreme Test of Power. Cape Town: Tafelberg.

Hough, M. "Die Konsep 'Indirect Strategie' Soos Deur André Beaufre Beskou". *ISSUP Strategic Review* (November 1980): 17–23.

Hough, M. "The Concept of 'Limited War' in Counter-insurgency". *ISSUP Strategic Review* (September 1983): 2–10.

Hough, M. "Some Policy and Strategic Aspects of the RSA White Paper on Defence and Armaments Supply". *ISSUP Strategic Review* (August 1982) 2–13.

Hough, M. "Revolutionary Warfare in the RSA". *ISSUP Strategic Review* (May 1986): 1–19.

Hough, M. "Revolutionary Targeting in the RSA Mobile Warfare in Southern Africa". *ISSUP Strategic Review* (May 1987): 1–20.

Kenney, Henry. 2016. *Verwoerd: Architect of Apartheid*. Jeppestown: Jonathan Ball Publishers (Pty) Ltd.

Knight, Ian. 1998. *Great Zulu Battles 1838–1906*. London: Orion Publishing Group Ltd.

Koorts, Lindie. 2014. D. F. Malan and the Rise of Afrikander Nationalism. Cape Town: NB Publishers.

Lopes, Manuel Martins. 1991. *A Problemática dos Conflitos Regionais*. Lisbon: Universitária Editora.

James III, W. Martin. 1992. *A Political History of the Civil War in Angola 1974–1990*. New Brunswick: Transaction Publishers.

Jana, Priscila. 2016. *Fighting for Mandela*. London: Metro Publishing.

Jeffery, Anthea. 2009. *People's War: New Light on the Struggle for South Africa*. Jeppestown: Jonathan Ball Publishers Pty Ltd.

Júnior, Miguel. "O Apartheid e a Guerra do Povo". *Jornal de Angola* (20 March 2012): 12.

(2014) *A Mão Sul-Africana O Envolvimento das Forças de Defesa da África do Sul no Sudeste de Angola 1966-1974*, Tribuna da História, Lisbon.

Macmillan, Hugh. 2014. *A Jacana Pocket Biography: Chris Hani*. Johannesburg: Jacana Media Pty Ltd.

Malan, Magnus and S. A. Weermag. "Die Aanslag Teen Suid-Africa". *ISSUP Strategic Review* (November 1980): 3–16.

Malan, Magnus. 2006. *My Life with the SA Defence Force*. Pretoria: Protea Book House.

Mandela, Nelson. 2006. *Longo Caminho para a Liberdade*. Porto: Campo das Letras Editores.

Melber, Henning. 2014. *Understanding Namibia*. Johannesburg: Jacana Media Pty Ltd.

Meredith, Martin. 2008. *Diamonds, Gold, and War: The Making of South Africa*. Jeppestown: Jonathan Ball Publishers Pty Ltd.

Mongiardim, Maria Regina. 2007. Coimbra: Diplomacia, Edições Almedina.

Onslow, Sue. 2009. Cold War in Southern Africa White Power, Black Liberation. New York: Routledge.

Pakenham, Thomas. 1998. *The Boer War*. London: Abacus Book.

Plessis, A du. "Diplomacy and Strategy: Patterns in the Diplomacy of Black Southern African States". *ISSUP Strategic Review* (March 1981): 2–13.

Plessis, A du. "South Africa and Regional Conflict Management: The Saliency of Informal and Secret Diplomacy". *ISSUP Strategic Review* (March 1984): 2–21.

Plessis, A du. "Just War Doctrine: Developments, Ramifications and Its Relevancy in the South African Context". *ISSUP Strategic Review* (May 1990): 14-–49.

Raftopoulos, Brian, and Alois Mlambo. 2014. *Becoming Zimbabwe*. Johannesburg: Jacana Media Pty Ltd.

Siko, John. 2014. *Inside South Africa's Foreign Policy*. New York: I. B. Taurus & Co. Ltd.

Sparks, Allister. 2003. *The Mind of South Africa: The Story of the Rise and Fall of Apartheid*. Jeppestown: Jonathan Ball Publishers Pty Ltd.

Sutter, Raymond. 2013. *ANC Underground in South Africa*. Johannesburg: Jacana Media Pty Ltd.

Tambo, Adelaide. 1987. *Oliver Tambo Speaks*. Cape Town: Kwela Books.

Terreblanche, Sampie. 2016. *A History of Inequality in South Africa 1652–2002*. Scottsville: University of KwaZulu-Natal Press.

Thompson, Leonard. 2014. A History of South Africa from the Earliest Known Human Inhabitation to the Present. Jeppestown: Jonathan Ball Publishers Pty Ltd.

Thomson, Alex. 2008. U.S. Foreign Policy Towards Apartheid South Africa: 1948-1994 Conflict of Interests. New York: Palgrave Macmillan.

Tombs, Robert. 2015. *The English and Their History*. UK: Penguin Books.

Venter, Al J. 2008. *How South Africa Built Six Atom Bombs*. Kyalami Estate: Ashanti Publishing.

Viljoen, C. L. "The Conventional Threat to the RSA and SWA". *ISSUP Strategic Review* (June 1983): 2–8.

Viljoen, C. L. "Revolutionary Warfare and Counter-Insurgency". *ISSUP Strategic Review* (ad hoc) 2–7.

Waag, Ian van der. 2015. *A Military History of Modern South Africa*. Jeppestown: Jonathan Ball Publishers Pty Ltd.

Walters, Ronald W. 1987. South Africa and the Bomb Responsibility and Deterrence. D. C. Heath and Company.

Welsh, David. (n.d.) *The Rise and Fall of Apartheid*. Jeppestown: Jonathan Ball Publishers Pty Ltd.

Welsh, Frank. 1998. *A History of South Africa*. London: HarperCollins Publishers.

Westhuizen, Christi van der. 2007. *White Power and the Rise and Fall of the National Party*. Cape Town: Zebra Press.

Wielligh, Nic von, and Lydia Wielligh-Steyn. 2014. *Die Bomb Suid-Afrika se Kernwapenprogam*. Pretoria: Uitegegee deur Litera Publikasies.

Wieder, Alan. 2013. *Ruth First and Joe Slovo in the War Against Apartheid*. Johannesburg: Jacana Media Pty Ltd.

Wilkins, Ivor, and Hans Strydom. 2014. *The Super Afrikaners Inside the Afrikaner Broederbond*. Jeppestown: Jonathan Ball Publishers Pty Ltd.

Wolvaardt, Pieter. 1999. *A Diplomat's Story: Apartheid and Beyond 1969-1998*, Alberton: Galago Books.

Official Documents of the Republic of South Africa

Oorsig oor Verdediging en Krygstuig Produksie Tydperk 1960 tot 1970. Republiek van Suid-Afrika.

White Paper on Defence 1965–1967. 1967. Cape Town: Republic of South Africa Defence Department.

White Paper on Defence and Armament Production 1969. 1969. Cape Town: Republic of South Africa Defence Department.

White Paper on Defence 1960–1970. 1970. Cape Town: Republic of South Africa Defence Department.

White Paper on Defence and Armament Production 1973. 1973. Cape Town: Republic of South Africa Defence Department.

White Paper on Defence 1977. 1977. Cape Town: Republic of South Africa Defence Department.

White Paper on Defence and Armaments Supply 1979. 1979. Cape Town: Republic of South Africa Defence Department.

White Paper on Defence and Armaments Supply 1982. 1982. Cape Town: Republic of South Africa Defence Department.

White Paper on Defence and Armament Supply 1984. 1984. Cape Town: Republic of South Africa Defence Department.

White Paper on the Planning Process of the South African Defence Force 1989. 1989. Cape Town: Republic of South Africa Defence Department.

Other Documents

Letter from South African President de Klerk to President Bush, Wilson Centre, Digital Archive International History, Declassified, 31 August 1990.

Report, South African Department of Foreign Affairs, "A Balanced Approach to the NPT: ARMSCOR/AEC Concerns Viewed from a DFA Standpoint", Wilson Centre, Digital Archive, International History, Declassified, 1 September 1988.

Speech by South African President F. W. de Klerk to a Joint Session of Parliament on Accession to the Non-Proliferation Treaty, Wilson Centre, Digital International History, Declassified, 24 March 1993.

South African Army Protection at Calueque and Alleged Invasion of Southern Angola, the Secretary for Foreign Affairs, Pretoria, Declassified, 3 September 1975.

Statement by the Minister of Defence, General Magnus Malan, News Release by Defence Headquarters, Pretoria, South Africa, 5 December 1985, Declassified, 5 February 2008.

Magazines of South Africa

ISSUP, S. N., Institute for Strategic Studies, University of Pretoria, 1978.

ISSUP, Institute for Strategic Studies, University of Pretoria, April 1979.

ISSUP, S. N., Institute for Strategic Studies, University of Pretoria, September 1979.

ISSUP, S.N., Institute for Strategic Studies, University of Pretoria, May 1980.

ISSUP, P 327.2, Institute for Strategic Studies, University of Pretoria, March 1981.

ISSUP, P 355.41, Institute for Strategic Studies, University of Pretoria, March 1982.

ISSUP, 355-43, Institute for Strategic Studies, University of Pretoria, June 1983.

ISSUP, 0250-1961, Institute for Strategic Studies, University of Pretoria, March 1983.

ISSUP, 0250-1961, Institute for Strategic Studies, University of Pretoria, June 1983.

ISSUP, 0250-1961, Institute for Strategic Studies, University of Pretoria, August 1987.

ISSUP, 1013-1108, Institute for Strategic Studies, University of Pretoria, November 1989.

ISSUP, 1013-1108, Institute for Strategic Studies, University of Pretoria, November 1990.
Militaria 17/2 1987
Paratus, March 1976.
Scientia Militaria, South African Journal of Military Studies, vol. 9, no. 1, 1–11, 1979.

About the Author

Miguel Júnior is a general officer of the Angolan armed forces and a military historian.